D1164225

THE CONSERVATION AND RESTORATION OF ANTIQUE FURNITURE

Stan Learoyd M.B.E.

 Sterling Publishing Co., Inc. New York

Published in 1983 by
Sterling Publishing Co., Inc.
Two Park Avenue
New York, N.Y. 10016

Phototypeset in 11 on 12 point Bembo by
Oliver Burridge and Company Limited
and printed in Great Britain by
BAS Printers Limited, Over Wallop, Hampshire.

ISBN 0-8069-7682-9

Published by arrangement with Evans Brothers Ltd.
This edition available in the United States, Canada and
the Philippine Islands only.

Contents

This book is dedicated to Remington Chesher who encouraged me to write and to Iris, my wife, who helped me.

Introduction

If the master restorer is to be completely competent at his trade, apart from his practical skills, he must be capable of closely dating the period when the piece of furniture he is restoring was made, and must also be able readily to recognise the various woods used. These two aspects alone can be almost a lifetime's study. It is not enough just to recognise that a timber is oak, walnut, mahogany, rosewood, or satinwood, etc., we must also identify the particular species. For example, American oak was not used in any quantity in England until about the mid-18th century, and the appearance, working quality, and finishing techniques for this wood are completely different from those of the European oaks.

In practice, the furniture restorer must first be a competent furniture maker, including chair-making, and must also have had experience in veneering by hand. He should be skilled in wood-turning and also in carving, have a thorough knowledge of gilding, decorative paintwork, and lacquer, but most important of all he should have a complete understanding of colouring, polishing, and finishing wood surfaces; more furniture is devalued by ignorance of these techniques than by any other restoration.

The restorer should be capable of working in brass, pewter, ivory, tortoiseshell, mother of pearl, etc., and should be able to mix and cast compo.

It is also necessary for the restorer to have a good knowledge of the development of upholstery through the different periods.

It will appear from this that the furniture restorer is expected to be a 'Jack of all trades', but this is not so. First and foremost he must be a skilled furniture constructor who has served an apprenticeship with a bespoke furniture maker, or the equivalent. The other skills required may be obtained by attending evening classes or short intensive group courses at technical colleges or similar institutions. Although he will not have the speed of the specialist craftsman, providing the tutors have commercial experience, he will quickly become sufficiently adept, so that together with practical workshop experience, he will be able to follow the detailed instructions in this manual and master any technique required in furniture conservation or restoration.

It may pay the master restorer to employ a polisher on a full-time basis, but unless the employee has had experience in antique furniture restoration, it will be necessary to advise and overlook the work that he will be doing as it is so different from modern polishing and colouring.

The small quantities of work in the other branches of furniture restoration usually make it uneconomic to employ a specialist, or to subcontract the work, unless the sub-contractor works nearby, so personal experience in these techniques is an advantage. If the business is large enough each one of the employees should be trained in at least one of these specialist subjects.

For upholstery work most restorers find that it is possible to employ a craftsman who has the necessary skill in traditional upholstery or to subcontract the work to him, but often it is necessary to give them guidance in the particular period style that is required.

Woods

Oak

The European oaks were mainly used in furniture construction until the end of the 18th century. Although a certain amount of American oak appears to have been imported from about the beginning of the 18th century, in the early days it was used almost entirely for interior construction.

The European oaks are interchangeable for repair work, providing care is taken to select timber which matches in texture and figure.

The American oaks are in two species, one red and one white, they are more fibrous in texture and not as easy to work as the European oaks. They will not fume, and for this reason alone they cannot be used in restoration as an alternative to European oak. In addition the cellular construction is closer and the medullary rays are liable to splinter and break away when the timber is quarter-cut, Fig. 1.

Bog oak which is dark brown, almost black in colour, was used mainly for inlaying, and was obtained from peat bogs where it had lain and been preserved for hundreds of years, hence the colour.

Pollard or Brown oak results from a fungus which distorts the natural growth of the tree and causes a certain amount of decay. This gives the timber a rich brown colour and it is mainly used for veneers and inlays.

Japanese oak was not imported into Europe until early in the 20th century. It is lighter in weight

Fig. 1 Timber sections, flat and quarter cut.

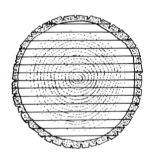

plain or flat cut is more liable to warp or twist than quartered.

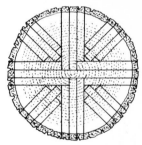

quarter cut to obtain maximum figure and ray display.

and colour and the medullary rays are smaller than other oaks.

Walnut

The European walnuts were certainly used for furniture making from the beginning of the 16th century on the Continent, but the walnut period of furniture making in England started about the middle of the 17th century.

Like the oaks, the European walnuts are interchangeable for repair work, but care must be taken in matching texture and figure. The American walnuts are completely different and cannot be used as an alternative to the European species, nor, obviously, can the European walnuts be used for repairs on furniture constructed in American walnut.

There are two groups of American walnut, the red or Virginian, which can be mistaken for mahogany by the inexperienced, and the black which is a dark, purple-brown with almost black streaks. Records show that American walnut was imported into Europe early in the 17th century, but came into general use in England in the latter part of the century, and appears to have lost favour by approximately the mid 18th century.

Burr walnut is mainly obtained from the butt or base of the tree, but is also found where there has been small multiple branch formations on the trunk.

Mahogany

There were only two species of mahogany in general use for furniture making up to approximately the beginning of the 19th century. The Spanish or Cuban mahogany from the West Indies was rich reddish-brown in colour and around 45lbs per cubic foot in weight, and Honduras mahogany from central America which was much lighter in colour and weight, approximately 30lbs per cubic foot. The latter came in much bigger widths and was most suitable for carcase construction.

A feature which is peculiar to these two mahoganies is a cream-coloured, close-grained, narrow line which follows, at approximately one inch intervals, the line of the figure where the spring and autumn grains meet, and this does not appear in any of the African mahoganies used in the 19th century. Another feature which is peculiar to Cuban mahogany, is that the grain appears to be filled with a white filler, and this should not be mistaken for the whitening used to fill the grain in African mahogany during the 19th century.

The African mahoganies, used from approximately 1800 are much more open-grained and coarser in appearance, and with practise it is not difficult to discern the difference between them and the two mahoganies used in the 18th century.

Satinwood

There are two distinct types of this wood, the West Indian and the East Indian, both are yellow in colour and vary in figure from plain to rich mottle.

The East Indian is more open-grained which gives it a cloudy brown appearance when polished. West Indian satinwood which is richer in colour was introduced into England around 1760 and the East Indian about 1800. The craftsmanship in satinwood furniture is usually of very high quality.

Rosewood

There are two varieties of this wood, the Brazilian which is purple-brown in colour with blackish, stripey grain, and the East Indian which is black to purple-brown in colour and is called 'blackwood' in its country of origin.

The colour plate endpapers in *English Furniture, Construction and Decoration* show the woods used for construction and for veneers in English period furniture.

Variations to the colours of timbers take place when they are exposed to daylight for a hundred years or more.

> European oaks will normally darken and enrich in colour
> American oaks will normally lighten in colour
> European walnut will lighten to a honey colour
> American walnut lightens to a purple-brown
> Cuban mahogany will lighten to honey colour
> Honduras mahogany will turn a pale cream colour
> Satinwood will fade but is more likely to retain its colour
> Rosewood will lighten in colour, but this is mainly caused by the polish on the surface bleaching

Sycamore will fade to light cream
Maple will darken to a yellow brown
Yew, cherry, chestnut and elm will lighten
Tulipwood will fade to pale pink and yellow

Kingwood will fade to a pale pink with a
hint of brown.
Other timbers though fading a little will
more or less retain their colour.

Cramps, jigs and special tools

Extra to the usual cramps, handscrews, etc., which the furniture maker would use, the restorer needs special jigs and gripping devices for many of the awkward cramping and holding jobs which he will have to deal with.

Rings cut from strong upholstery coil springs are useful for holding small pieces of carving, moulding, facings, etc., in position until the glue has set, Fig. 2. The cut ends should not be filed smooth because they will grip better left rough and any slight damage caused can easily be corrected. A piece of wood can be put under the ends when using them on flat polished surfaces.

When cramping shaped and circular frame work, use a length of strong, wide upholsterer's webbing, about 45in long, with hardwood blocks glued and tacked on each end on which the handscrews will grip when it is in use. Fig. 3 shows the web cramp in use with handscrews cramping up the seat frame of a roundbacked chair. If the back head rail were round it would also be used for fixing that, with the handscrews gripped on the seat rails. An upholsterer's web stretcher, Fig. 4, can be used instead of gluing blocks on the end of the webbing. Thread the webbing into the stretcher, doubled so that it forms a loop to go round the shaped frame.

Wood bench clip, Fig. 5, is used for holding panels, pilasters, etc., on the bench when handscrews would interfere with easy working. The lower end of the screwhole is slotted so that

Web stretcher used for cramping shaped seat frame.

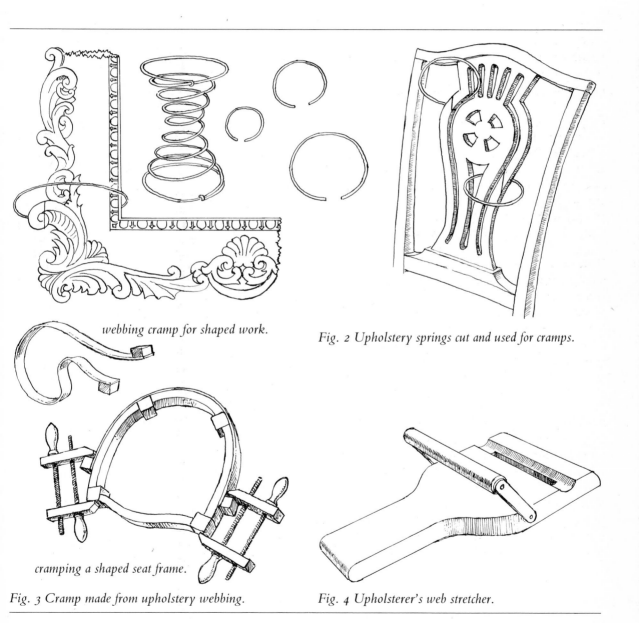

webbing cramp for shaped work.

Fig. 2 Upholstery springs cut and used for cramps.

cramping a shaped seat frame.

Fig. 3 Cramp made from upholstery webbing.

Fig. 4 Upholsterer's web stretcher.

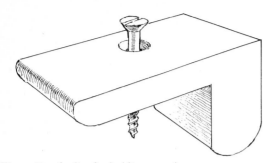

Fig. 5 Bench clip for holding panels.

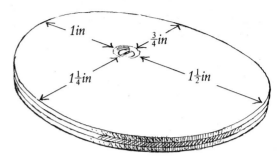

Fig. 7 Plywood cam bench stop used in conjunction with normal bench stop when dressing frames or panels.

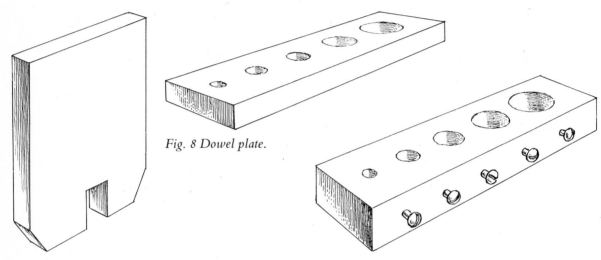

Fig. 8 Dowel plate.

Fig. 6 Wood jaw-facing for bar cramp.

Fig. 9 Dowel groover.

various thicknesses of timber can be held with the screw always in a vertical position.

Plywood blocks should be fitted on bar or sash cramps to prevent the jaws damaging the wood surface. If they are slotted to fit snugly over the bar, Fig. 6, they will hold in position when in use and can easily be removed if desired. When gluing up a chair frame or similar job, where the cramp is gripping at an angle of more than 90 degrees, lightly damp the wood jaws with water to reduce the danger of the jaw sliding off the polished surface.

A paper-board (a flat softwood board with a layer of paper glued on its face) is used to glue on small pieces for carving, etc., which would

otherwise be difficult to hold. When cutting frets this is the best method for holding them, and using carving tools to cut them gives a much cleaner finish than a fret saw. There is much less danger of damage or breakage and no further attention is needed after cutting. The work can easily be removed when completed by sliding a thin knife blade under it, see page 126.

A pivoting-cam bench stop, Fig. 7, is used in conjunction with the normal bench stop to hold panels, etc., tight while they are being dressed and cleaned. If there is a German end vice on the bench this would not be necessary, of course.

A dowel plate, Fig. 8, made of steel with various size holes bored through it is used to make dowels

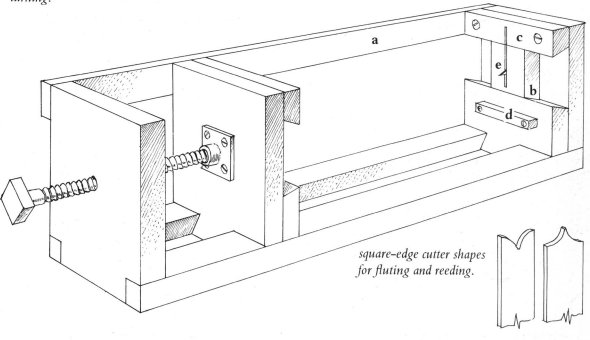

Fig. 10 Fluting and reeding jig for square or turned, parallel or tapered legs, etc.

a *Straight-edge guide for scratch-stock;* **b** *Slide, used when working square section legs only;* **c** *Block traps slide when screws are tightened;* **d** *Bottom rest for legs, etc., removed when working turned leg with top square block;* **e** *Positioning pin, set central on turning.*

square-edge cutter shapes for fluting and reeding.

of a special size. By using straight-grained timber, roughly dressed to the size required, and driving it through the plate the dowels are made accurate to size and shape.

A dowel groover, Fig. 9, is necessary when replacing dowel in damaged dowel joints. A hardwood block is bored with holes to fit the various sizes of dowels and screws are put in central at both sides of each hole. Their points should just protrude through the face of the dowel holes. When a dowel is driven through the appropriate hole, a groove is made on each side of it by the screw points. When the dowel is driven into the joint, the surplus glue and air is released through the grooves instead of accumulating at the bottom of the hole or being

forced through the grain of the timber and possibly splitting it.

A special holding jig, Fig. 10, is needed when flutes, reeds or inlays have to be worked on turnings or tapered and square legs. With the guide of the scratch-stock laid tight up to the straight edge on the side of the jig (the straight edge should be adjustable for tapered legs), the cutter will work the necessary shape accurately down the centre of the leg. The cutters should be square-edged, not bevelled like a chisel or plane iron, and should be about the same thickness as a cabinet scraper. The cutters for reeding and fluting must be shaped as shown so that when tapered legs are being worked the taper on the flutes and reeds will correspond to the taper on the turning.

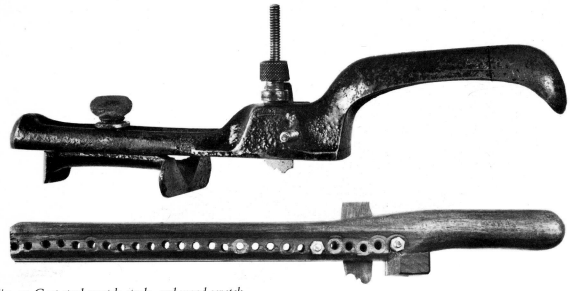

Fig. 11 Cast steel scratch-stock, and wood scratch-stock.

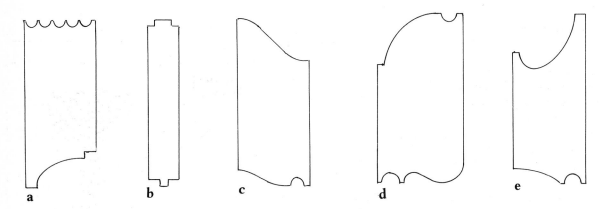

a   b   c   d   e

Fig. 12 Scratch-stock cutters.

a *Multi-reeding ovalo;* **b** *Line-inlay, stringing, routing;* **c** *Ogee, ogee and bead, reverse-repeat leg mould;* **d** *Scotia and bead, ogee and bead, reverse-repeat leg mould;* **e** *Thumb mould, round and bead, reverse-repeat leg mould.*
The shapes shown can be cleanly and easily worked with a scratch-stock, but it is advisable only to make them as and when they are required. Needle files may be used to shape the cutters, but to get a clean finish slip stones should finally be used on the square cutter edge, and the two faces of the cutter should be burnished on a flat oilstone.

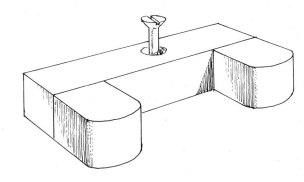

Fig. 13 Special guide used on scratch-stock for serpentine and circular work.

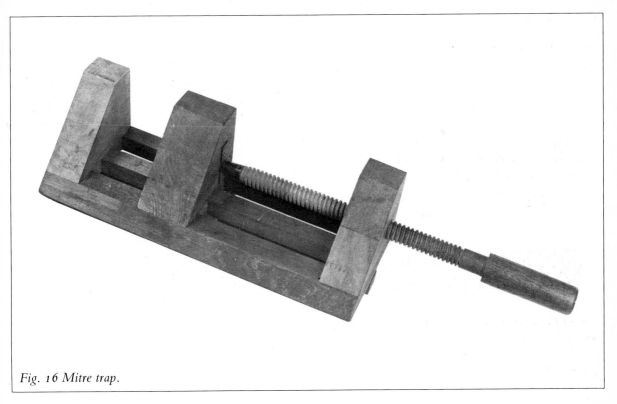

Fig. 16 Mitre trap.

A cast-steel or wood scratch-stock, which can be made by the craftsman himself, is necessary for moulding, Fig. 11. A selection of the kind of cutters which may be required is shown in Fig. 12 and these should only be made as needed. A special guide is used on the scratch-stock for circular work, Fig. 13.

A leather-faced mallet is necessary for Buhl work. Fig. 14 shows one made with a roll of leather gripped in a metal tube and the other is a small wood mallet converted by a piece of leather glued on to the face.

A selection of syringes is required ranging from old medical hypodermics for fine injections to engineer's grease guns with reduced outlet holes, Fig. 15.

A mitre trap has various uses but its main purpose is for shooting mitres and squaring ends on bollection moulds, etc. It can be made with either a metal or a wood screw which is threaded into the end block and fixed so that it will turn on the centre sliding block, Fig. 16.

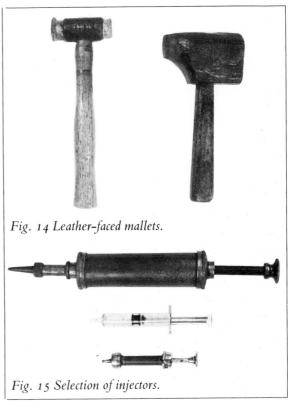

Fig. 14 Leather-faced mallets.

Fig. 15 Selection of injectors.

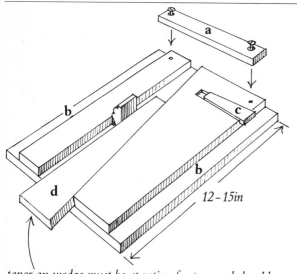

Fig. 17 Bench hook.

a *Screwed on when using shooting board;* **b** *Plane beds when using shooting board;* **c** *Stop used when dressing veneers, it is removed when not in use;* **d** *Wedge-vice holds small pieces and can be used when moulding with scratch-stock, the scratch-stock guide works on the shooting face* **b**

12-15in

taper on wedge must be at ratio of 4 to 1 and should be slightly under cut on tapered edge to stop it rising.

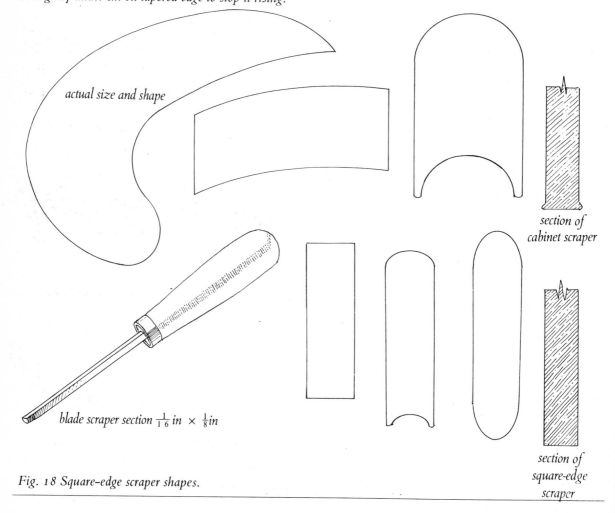

actual size and shape

section of cabinet scraper

blade scraper section $\frac{1}{16}$ in $\times$ $\frac{1}{8}$ in

section of square-edge scraper

Fig. 18 Square-edge scraper shapes.

Fig. 19 Die-maker's rifflers.

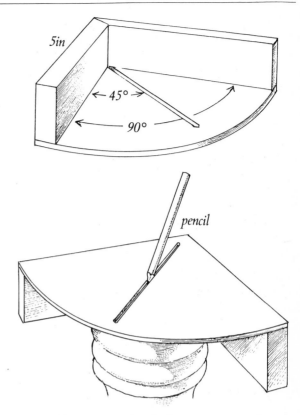

Fig. 20 Turner's centring jig for square or round section timber.

The special bench hook, Fig. 17, is used for clamping small pieces when the vice is already in use. It can also be used for shooting, veneer dressing and, when reversed, for sawing.

A selection of square-edged scrapers shown in Fig. 18 are used for Buhl, marquetry and dressing carvings. They can also be used for stripping surplus glue from joints.

A selection of die-maker's riffler files are needed for use on Buhl, marquetry and shaped work, Fig. 19.

Jig made in the workshop and used to centre ends of rounds or squares for turnings, Fig. 20.

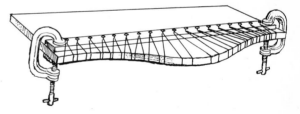

Fig. 21 Pin boards and twine for cramping shaped edges.

Pin-boards and upholsterers' twine, Fig. 21, are used for cramping crossbands, moulds, etc. on circular work. After tightly threading the twine round the pins and over the edge to be fixed, the twine should be damped which will make it shrink and draw even tighter.

Nosed side-cutting pliers, Fig. 22, are useful for removing nails and screws which cannot be gripped with pincers.

Fig. 22 Nosed side-cutting pliers.

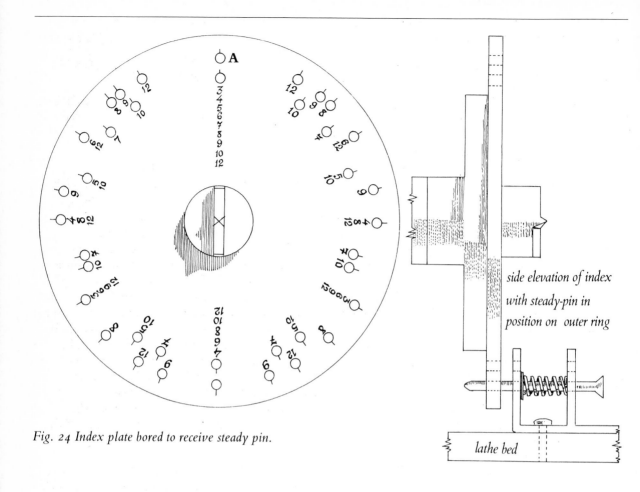

side elevation of index
with steady-pin in
position on outer ring

lathe bed

Fig. 24 Index plate bored to receive steady pin.

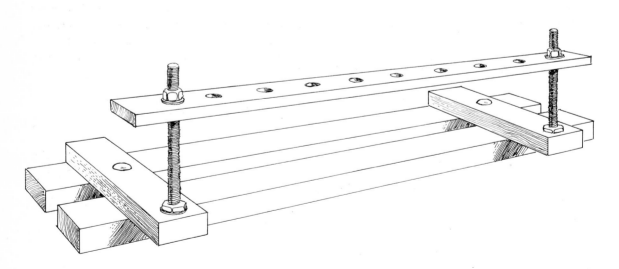

Fig. 25 Straight-edge jig fitted on lathe-bed for fluting and reeding, etc.

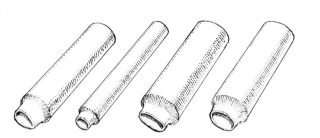

Fig. 23 Veneer repair punches.

Fig. 26 Dowel pops.

Veneer-cutting punches can be made from steel tubing by bevelling off the outside edge of the tube until the inside edge gives a fine clean cut. The bevel should be long enough to cause the minimum of bruising-back of the top edge of the veneer. The tubes need not be left round in section, they can be hammered into various shapes, Fig. 23. They are used when replacing small areas of damaged or missing burr veneer. The new piece of veneer and the hole to receive it are, of course, cut with the same punch. The punches used by the saddler and in the leather trade are an alternative to home-made punches.

Fig. 24 shows an index plate for the lathe which can be used for reeding and fluting legs instead of the special holding jig, Fig. 10. The plate can be made from metal or wood and is bolted to the lathe faceplate. The figures against the bored holes give the number of sections into which the circumference of the turning can be divided. The steady pin is put in to the hole at A, on the inner

or outer circle of holes depending on the divisions required and then subsequently into each hole which is numbered with the divisions required. For example, if eight divisions are required the pin would be put in the outside hole at A and after working the reed or groove on the top centre of the turning the lathe would then be moved round until the pin entered the next hole marked with the number eight, repeating the operation until the pin has been in all the holes marked with an eight. The scratch-stock is guided by fixing a straight-edge on the lathe making sure that it is parallel to the centres of the lathe Fig. 25.

Dowel-pops, Fig. 26 can be used for positioning dowels in a joint where it would be impossible to mark their position with a gauge. One half of the joint is bored and the pops are then placed in the holes to mark the other half. The pops can be made of brass or mild steel, and can be turned on the lathe.

Constructional repairs

Worm-weakened wood may be strengthened by the following method. Mix animal glue size to a jelly-like consistency in a container large enough to submerge the timbers completely. With the size at body heat, approximately 100°F, soak the timber in it for between twenty minutes and half an hour, not longer or hotter or it will cause surface cracking. Remove and lay it on paper until the glue has set. Do not remove any of the surface glue until it has set; it will then wipe off quite easily from the polished surfaces and it need not be removed from the unpolished areas.

Do not remove any of the worm dust before starting the operation because it acts like blotting paper, soaking up the size into the timber, and acting as a filler.

If the timbers are too large to submerge in a vat, lay them on a horizontal surface with the unpolished side uppermost (if polished on both sides the least important side must be stripped). With the size almost at boiling point (it must not be allowed to boil) apply it liberally to the surface with a firm brush and force it into the grain by working over it with a warm, not hot, electric clothes iron or flat iron. Repeat the process until it is obvious that the timber will not receive any more size and then cover with paper and lay on one side until it sets.

This worm treatment should be done before starting on the repairs, but if a new piece of timber has to be fitted to replace a missing part, for example a tenon, the joint can be roughly prepared with saw or chisel. The final fitting should be left until the size has been applied and allowed to set so that the joint can be worked cleanly without any of the worm-eaten wood breaking away.

This treatment will usually make the timber as strong as it was originally and often avoids having to replace parts with new timber which will devalue the piece, a fact which should always be taken into consideration.

Glues
For all normal rejointing and veneering the animal glue (in cake, or pearl form) is the kind which should be used, because it is easier to break-down again if a restorer at some future date, requires to take the joint apart for other repairs, and for furniture it is just as strong as the synthetic glues. These synthetic glues may be used, if preferred, where breakages occur other than joints, or where new pieces have to be spliced in.

CHAIR AND STOOL REPAIRS

Before starting any repair work dismantle all loose joints. These should, of course, have been noted when the original examination was made. Loose seat rail joints are a common occurrence, mainly because people will rock a chair or stool on to its back legs thus putting a terrific strain on the joints. If the chair or stool has a stuff-over seat, with the upholstery covering the rails, this should be removed first, taking care to keep it in its original order as far as possible, so making replacement easier. This particularly applies if it is an original stuffing. If a joint is firm, but it is necessary to take it apart to be able to dismantle

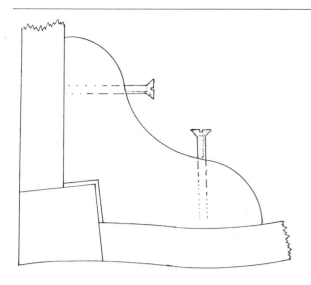

Fig. 28 When gluing and fixing blocks, screws must be at right-angles to the joints.

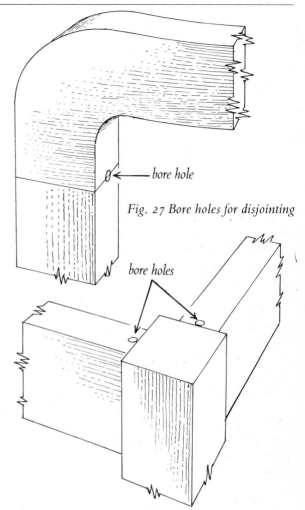

bore hole

Fig. 27 Bore holes for disjointing

bore holes

other loose joints, bore a fine hole through the top edge of the joint central to the shoulder and over the tenon and with a fine syringe, which fits snugly into the hole, inject methylated spirit. This will circulate round the tenon joint and crystalise the old glue making it possible to tap the joint apart without creating any further damage, Fig. 27. When tapping joints apart use a fairly heavy hammer, about 2lbs, and a block of wood, rather than a mallet which is more likely to cause damage. If it is necessary to take a chair frame back to pieces, and one or both of the head rail joints are firm, turn the chair on its side and bore a hole in the inside edge of the joint at the shoulder to inject the methylated spirit.

Blocks can be removed from seat frames by applying methylated spirit at the angle where the block meets the rail. It should be left for a few seconds before tapping off the block which should then come away without any trouble. Blocks should fit firmly into the angles if any real benefit is to be gained from them, and if the original blocks are a bad fit and cannot be made to fit well, they should be replaced with new ones. This is one of the few replacements which can be done without devaluing the piece of furniture. It is often necessary to prepare the rails before fitting the blocks, Fig. 28.

Metal plates which have been used for repair work, should always be removed and replaced by wood. It is impossible to have a perfect joint between metal and wood, because there is opposing expansion and contraction between the two. Also the fact that screws or nails have to be used to fix the metal contribute to a likelihood of further damage.

When re-gluing chair frames it is usual to glue up the front and back first, the exception being Regency sabre-leg chairs which should have the sides glued first. When gluing up chair and stool frames with straight rails ordinary bar cramps are used to get a direct pull to close the joints. If the rails are shaped the bar cramps will not give a direct pull and may cause a joint to break. Instead a webbing cramp should be used, Fig. 3,

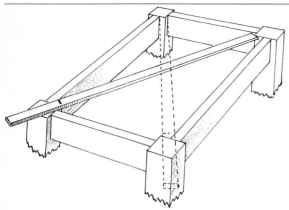

Fig. 29 Lath used across diagonals when squaring frames.

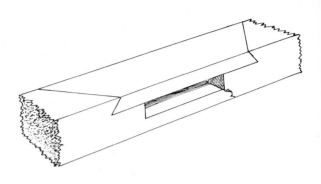

Fig. 30 Piece spliced into broken back chair leg, after first gluing together the break.

page 13. After a chair has been glued together the seat frame should be checked to make sure that it is clear of twist by casting an eye over the side or front rails, and also square by using a squaring lath, Fig. 29. Adjust the cramps until both are correct. If the chair has a loose, upholstered seat this too should be tested to make sure it fits, but it should not be left in when the chair is being glued up. Often extra covers have been added which makes them bigger and this may be why the joints have been forced apart. If this is so, the covers will have to be removed and the seat re-upholstered.

When the chair back is broken, which often occurs at seat rail level, the back legs must be completely disjointed, and the break glued back together again, making sure that it is fitting tight back in its original position. Any new pieces may then be cut and fitted on the back and side faces of the legs. The depth should be only to the outside face of the mortice hole, and long enough to be at least 1in clear of the break and mortice hole. Make sure that when fitting the new piece, no part is butt jointed, end grain to end grain, Fig. 30. If perfect joints are made the chair back will be as strong as it was originally. This type of jointing can be applied to any part of a square section leg with the pieces cut to a depth of about $\frac{1}{4}$in unless it is a long, angled clean break following the grain of the wood. It could then just be glued and rub-jointed and should be as strong or stronger than it was originally. Under no circumstances should nails or screws be used

to help fix joints. They only weaken the timber and the expansion of the metal causes splitting.

If a cabriole leg is broken and fits together perfectly, but is too short in the grain to be strong by simple re-gluing, drive a fine panel pin into one half of the broken face at a position where it is strongest. Cut off the head to leave no more than $\frac{1}{8}$in above the surface. Take the other half of the leg and press the two halves of the break carefully together making sure that they fit accurately. Draw apart and remove the pin which has now marked the centre for a drill to be used to bore for a dowel. When boring make certain that the bore is parallel to the back faces of the leg. The dowel should not be more than one third of the thickness of the leg at the break and should be grooved so that surplus glue can be released (see Fig. 9, page 14).

If a leg, particularly a cabriole leg, is so badly shattered that it is necessary to joint in a new section, first make an outline drawing on ply or cardboard using, if possible, one of the perfect legs, by laying it face uppermost and marking round its outline, Fig. 31. The two halves of the broken leg can now be prepared for the new piece to be joined on to them. Make the two halves of the joint as parallel as possible to each other, and if the break is straight across the grain it should be recut to make an angle of at least 45 degrees for strength. Lay the leg accurately on to the pattern, and take the measurements for the new piece required. The new piece should be

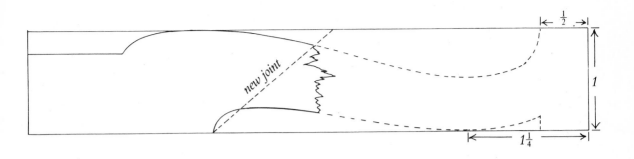

Fig. 31 Card pattern when restoring part of cabriole leg.

cut at least ⅛in oversize all ways to allow for fitting. Glue the new piece to the upper half of the leg making sure it is a perfect fit, and holding it in position with one or more spring clips until the glue has set. The reason for gluing to the upper half first is because it is easier to grip in the vice when fitting. The unglued face of the new timber can now be dressed down until both halves, when fitted together and laid on the pattern, fit the outline accurately whichever of the back two faces of the leg are laid on to it. With the two halves accurately in position on the pattern, mark round the lower part of the leg on to the face of the new timber to ensure that you get it in the right place when gluing it on. Now glue the two halves together holding the upper half in the vice. Use spring clips again to hold the joint in position and check the leg with the pattern before leaving it to set. When the glue is set the surplus timber on the new section can be dressed and levelled with chisels, spokeshaves and finally with the comma-shaped square-edge scraper (see Fig. 18, page 18).

If the lower part of a cabriole leg has been cut off or is broken and missing, a card pattern should be made. First cut the card to the width of the thickest part of the leg (from the knee to the face where the wing-block is fixed; this would be the size of the timber from which the leg was originally cut). Now lay the original part of the leg with the top end to one end of the pattern, and the square edge, where the wing and rail join it, tight up to the edge of the pattern and

mark round its outline on to the card. With a straight-edge laid to the back line of the leg shape draw a continuation of this line until it meets the edge of the card. From this point measure down one and a quarter times the width of the card pattern (or one and a quarter times the width of the timber from which the leg was cut) and this will give the approximate length of the original leg if it was made with a pad foot. If it was a ball and claw, lion paw, or scroll foot, one and three quarter times the width should be added. If the leg is off a dining chair a second check can be made. The overall length of the leg would be approximately seventeen inches. The original part of the leg can now be prepared for jointing making the splice as long as possible. Lay the part leg accurately on the pattern and measure the length of the new piece required allowing at least an extra ½in in length for fitting, but the width and thickness must be accurate to the overall width of the card pattern.

Now cut and fit the joint for the new section until the old section can be laid in position on the card pattern on either of its back faces, and the new section, when laid so that it fits over the lower part of the card, will make a perfect joint on either face, Fig. 31. Glue and rub joint the two parts together and check them on the pattern to make sure they are correctly positioned. Then apply spring clips (see Fig. 2, page 13) to hold them until the glue sets. For marking out the shape, cutting on the band saw or jigsaw and final finishing, see chapter on carving.

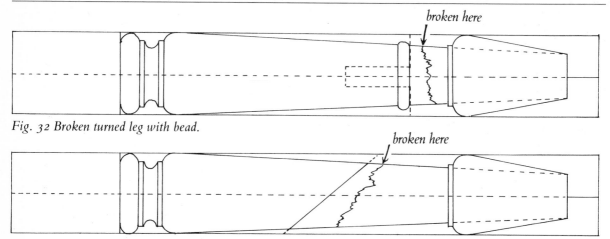

broken here

Fig. 32 Broken turned leg with bead.

broken here

Fig. 33 Broken turned leg with splice and no bead.

Turned legs which have been broken or reduced in length may be restored in two ways.

If the leg has a protruding bead or member at a position where a minimum of the original leg will be lost, the leg can be cut back to within approximately $\frac{1}{8}$in of this bead, Fig. 32. The new face should be centred using the special jig shown on page 19, Fig. 20, and set up in the lathe with the new face fitted at the end stock, not at the driving stock. The face can then be turned down until it is flush to the side of the bead or member. The new face should then be bored to receive a dowel pin which should not be more than one third of the thickness of the leg at the joint. The new section of the leg can now be prepared. In length it must be at least $\frac{1}{4}$in longer than the net length required plus the length of the pin, and $\frac{1}{4}$in oversize in width and thickness. Put in the lathe and work it into a round, turning the dowel pin at the same time. Now glue the old and the new parts together and when the glue has set, put it in the lathe again and complete the new part in detail. The dowel pin should always be grooved on each side so that air and surplus glue is released from the hole.

The second method is used when a leg has no suitable bead or member where a joint with a dowel pin can be used and the new piece must be spliced on to the old, Fig. 33. A butt joint, square across the grain, should never be used. First make a cardboard pattern by cutting the

card to the width of the square of the leg. Lay the original part of the leg centrally on it and mark accurately round the outline, using calipers if necessary to make sure the widths are correct. Now lay a straight-edge along the two side lines of the shape marked on the pattern and extend them as required (if a dining chair, to approximately seventeen inches overall). If it decided that the original had a tapered toe called an Adam toe on it, and this can often be decided by the smallness of width at the bottom point of the leg, then this toe should be drawn on to the pattern. The height will be approximately one and a half times the overall width of the pattern. Its top end will be approximately the width of the pattern and the taper will finish at the same point as the continuation of the leg taper. The original part of the leg should now be prepared for splicing. The longer the splice is the stronger it will be, but it should never be less than 45 degrees. It is best to make the splice to the back of the leg. Measure for the new section by laying the original on the pattern in its correct position and measure from the top end of the splice to the bottom of the foot. The new piece should be cut at least $\frac{1}{4}$in longer than this measurement, and the width and thickness should also be $\frac{1}{4}$in oversize. Splice the old and the new parts together, making sure that they line up correctly with the pattern. Glue and rub joint them together using spring clips to hold them until the glue has set. Draw a line accurately through the centre of the leg pattern and lay the

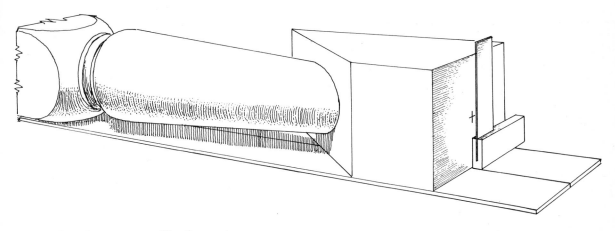

Fig. 34 Centring new part of leg for turning.

leg on it in its correct position. Using a set-square vertically from the central pattern line, mark a line on the bottom end of the foot. Turn the leg over 90 degrees and repeat the operation with the set-square. The centre on the new part is now marked ready for turning in the lathe. This method of centring with the set-square ensures that it lines up with the original part of the leg, Fig. 34. The centre of the new part may be slightly out because of the jointing. The leg can now be set up in the lathe and turned, but care should be taken when turning the section at the splice, that the original part of the leg is not marked by the chisels. It is better to do the final levelling at the joint with a fine spokeshave to avoid destroying the original surface. It is almost certain that the old part of the leg will not be a true round, because of shrinkage.

Broken joints on chairs are a common problem for the restorer. If the top square of a front leg is shattered where the tenons enter it, the leg should not be renewed. It should carefully be disjointed from the chair and all the cracks glued together. All missing pieces should be replaced and if this is carefully done it should be as strong as it was originally. The reason why it was broken in the first place was probably because the joints fitted badly or had not been thoroughly glued. If the former, then glue thin veneers on the tenons to make them fit. Sometimes damage is caused by inexperienced people fixing loose joints with nails or screws. These should always

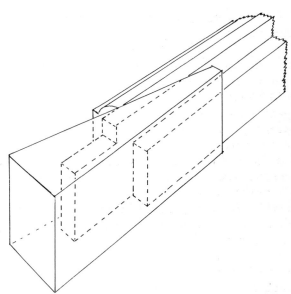

Fig. 35 Piece spliced on rail for new tenon.

be removed and the holes filled with wood.

If a tenon has broken off, it is not normally possible to satisfactorily glue it on again because it would be fixing end grain to end grain. The break is usually as a result of weakening by woodworm, or use of cross-grained timber. A new piece of timber should be fixed on the inside face of the rail with the longest splice possible, with an extension beyond the shoulder on which the new tenon can be cut, Fig. 35. First strengthen the worm-weakened timber; as described on page 22 for worm treatment. The

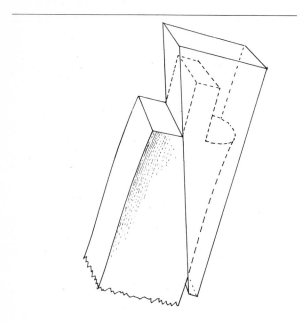

Fig. 36 Piece spliced on leg for new tenon.

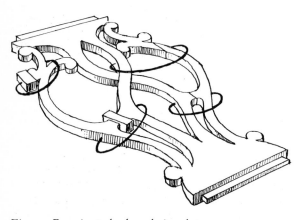

Fig. 37 Repairs to broken chair splat.

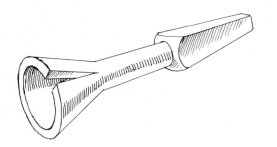

Fig. 38 Dowel rounder bit.

splice should be rub-jointed and held with spring clips until the glue is set. Screws or nails should never be used to hold a joint. They only cause further weakening of the timber. If a tenon is broken on the back leg where it joins the head rail, it should be spliced out on the back face of the leg, Fig. 36. Head rails which are damaged at the leg mortice joint or at the splat plough should be restored by the same method used for the upper part of a front leg, by gluing loose pieces and cracks carefully back in position, and splicing pieces in any area where parts are missing. Spring clips can be used for holding parts when necessary.

When repairing a damaged back splat first make sure all cracks and joints are clean before gluing, and when glued hold together with spring clips until set. When parts are missing and a plane can be used for preparing the joint, a fine mouth block or bullnose plane should be used. If the opening is too narrow for a plane a sharp chisel should be used to trim the two faces between which the new piece is to be fitted. Taper the opening from front to back, so that the new piece will be slightly wedge-shaped. Care should be taken to make sure that the grain of any new piece is running in the same way as the rest of the splat. They should be rub-jointed into position and spring clips used to hold them if necessary, Fig. 37.

Broken dowel joints usually require the removal of the old dowels. First, any other damage to the joint should be repaired and then the old dowels can be removed by dressing them off level to the joint and marking their centres as near as possible with a centre punch. With a drill approximately two-thirds the size of the dowel, bore out the centre of the dowel ($\frac{3}{8}$in dowel = $\frac{1}{4}$in drill), then with a small gouge, the surplus dowel can be split off into the central hole and removed. Make sure that a groove is worked on opposite sides of the dowel to release air and glue, see Fig. 9, page 14, and that the top edges are chamfered, preferably with a dowel-rounder bit, Fig. 38, before fitting the new dowel.

Broken head rail joints on chairs, when the head rail extends beyond the legs, are usually slot dovetailed to receive the legs and through shrinkage or clumsy handling are often splintered at the joints. First remove the head rail, using methylated spirits to release it if necessary, and then cut away the damaged area. If the damage is on the outside part of the rail, cut right to outside edges; if the damage is inside the leg, cut at an angle of 45 degrees where the jointing is end grain to end grain. Use a bullnose plane in preference to a chisel wherever possible to get perfect surfaces on which the new timber is to be fitted. With the head rail cramped in its original position on the legs, fit the new pieces making sure that the angle is correct where it fits up to the dovetail on the leg. The head rail can now be removed from the legs and the new pieces glued in position. When the glue is set, the new parts can be dressed and levelled to the original and the head rail glued back in position on the legs, Fig. 39.

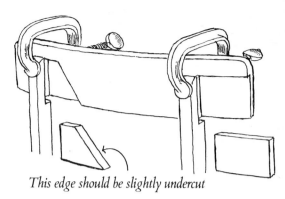

This edge should be slightly undercut

Fig. 39 Restoring a damaged chair headrail.

CARCASSES

Early frame carcasses

The mortice and tenon joints on carcasses of early period furniture were dry-jointed and pinned, and as a result of shrinkage have often worked loose. Sometimes the pins extend beyond the back face of the framing and may be tapped out easily, but if they are flush or below the back face, a parallel metal punch, in diameter two-thirds of the size of the pins with the end ground concave, may be used to remove them. If neither of these methods can be used to remove the pins, for example when the pins do not penetrate the back face, use the technique for removing broken dowels described on page 28. It is usually necessary to fit new pins because the original ones have been strained and worn, and the bore through the tenon has been enlarged. Before fitting the new pins, the hole on the face side of the mortice hole should be slightly enlarged so that any wear which has taken place in the pin hole of the tenon can be filled by the slightly thicker pins. The pins should be chamfered at their points and should also be slightly tapered so that when they are driven in they draw the shoulders of the joint tight up to the stiles. Care should be taken not to split the end of the tenon

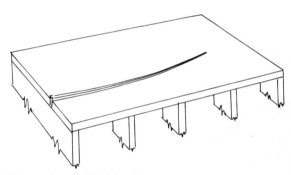

Fig. 40 Crack filled by skiver.

by having too much taper on the pins or by driving them in too firmly. The mortice and tenon joints may be glued, which will make them hold more firmly than if they are dry-jointed. If tenons are broken or missing, pieces should be spliced on and new ones cut as described on page 27.

If panels are split they should be rejointed with glue and if, as a result of shrinkage, they are too narrow to fit into both ploughs, a piece should be jointed on to the outside edge where it will be least noticeable. The same procedure will apply to solid tops, but if it is not possible for some reason to remove the top then the crack should be filled with a wood skiver (a lath of matching timber split, not sawn) carefully fitted into the front face of the crack and then glued and dressed level, Fig. 40.

Solid timber carcasses

The use of solid timber and dovetail jointing in carcasses of the later periods (in England, circa 1680) lessened the possibility of the carcasses becoming unfirm, but damage caused by shrinkage was more prevalent, resulting in cracked carcase sides, and veneer facings on carcase edges at rail joints being forced off and shattered, Fig. 41 and 42. In the walnut period the carcase sides were ploughed to receive the drawer runners and the ends of the drawer rails, and a veneer of walnut was glued on the front edges of the sides to cover the joints, Fig. 41. In the early 18th century the square plough was replaced by a slot dovetail, Fig. 42. In the early period, because the drawer runners were glued into the plough and were made with their grain running from the front to the back of the carcase, the result was that although the carcase sides shrank in width, the runners did not shrink and therefore the sides cracked. Also the veneers were forced and splintered at the rail joints. By removing the drawer runners, the cracks in the ends can usually be glued and closed again, but because by doing this the sides are reduced in width, the depth for the drawers or shelves, etc., is also reduced, which could result in having to reduce all of them, or increase the carcase sides by gluing a strip on the back edge. An alternative to closing the cracks is to fill them with a wood skiver (a lath split or riven off a straight-grained board). The grain will then follow the grain of the sides. If the skivers have to be jointed in length they should be mitred not square butted. They should be planed with a slight taper to make them easy to enter into the cracks, and care should be taken before finally driving them home, so that the carcase faces on each side of the crack are level to each other, Fig. 40.

Restoring carcase facings

If they are cross-banded (the grain running across the thickness of the edges) any new piece can be jointed in, with square ends where it joins the original, Fig. 41, but care must be taken to make sure that the grain is running the same way as the original (see Preparing and Patching Veneers), otherwise it will be almost impossible to colour match. If the carcase facings are straight-grained, not cross-banded the joins between the new and

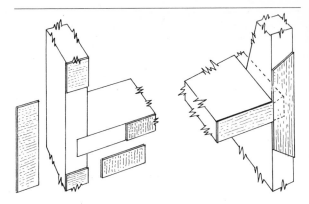

Fig. 41 Plough joint with cross-band facings.

Fig. 42 Slot-dovetail joint with straight grain facings.

the original must be mitred to make a more perfect joint, Fig. 42. This makes them easier to blend together when colouring and polishing. Make sure, also, that the grain of the new is in the same direction as the original.

RESTORING INTERIORS

Drawers

Worn drawer runners fixed on the underside of the drawers will often need renewing if the drawers are going to run in and out smoothly. If the drawer bottoms are ploughed into the sides, Fig. 43, remove the blocks only and replace them with new ones of the correct thickness (the top edge of the drawer side should fit neatly under the rail above the drawer), but they should be about one and a half times the width of the originals to give extra sliding surface. If the grain of the drawer bottom is running from front to back, Fig. 46, it will probably need rejointing and pieces added to make up for any shrinkage. The new runners can be made in one length and glued to the underside of the drawer bottom and to what is left of the extension of the drawer sides. If so desired by the customer, for appearance sake, a skiver can now be fitted in the angle between the blocks and the drawer sides to make up for the worn bottoms of the sides but the drawers should work quite well without doing this. If the bottoms are rebated into the sides, the new blocks can be fitted flush to the outside face of the drawer sides, Fig. 44.

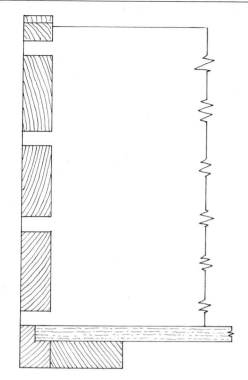

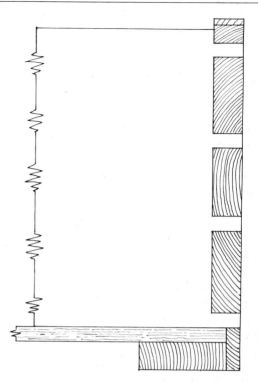

Fig. 43 Drawer back section with ploughed side.

Fig. 44 Drawer back section with rebated side.

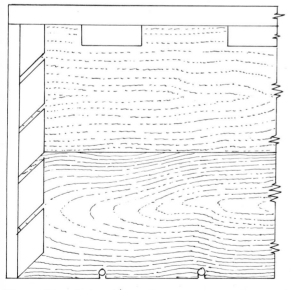

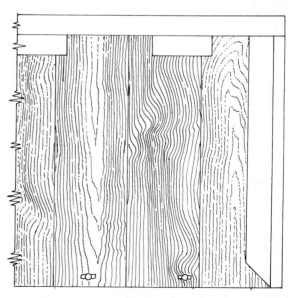

Fig. 45 Ploughed-in drawer bottom with grain from side to side.

Fig. 46 Rebated-in drawer bottom with grain front to back.

If the grain of the drawer bottoms is running from side to side, Fig. 45, remove the blocks, and after jointing up the drawer bottoms if required, fit new blocks. Instead of making them in one piece, make them up of short pieces mitred together but spaced about $\frac{1}{16}$ in apart, which will allow the bottoms to shrink or swell without splitting. If the drawer bottoms are ploughed into the sides the blocks should be glued to the bottoms only, and blocks should be glued along the front edge of the bottoms to hold them in the front plough. The holes for the nails or screws which fix the bottoms to the backs should be slotted to allow for shrinkage, etc.

Drawer bottom repairs will vary according to the value of the furniture and some pieces may not justify removing cracked bottoms and rejointing them. An alternative is to fill them with wood skivers but this also may be too expensive. They should not, however, be left untouched because something might wedge in the crack and trap the drawer, so cover them with a strip of blind-holland glued on the top surface.

Worn runners on the carcase on which the drawers are supported will vary in construction. If they are simply pieces approximately 2in × 1in in section glued into the ploughed carcase sides, or glued and nailed or screwed on to the sides without ploughs, they can be removed by injecting methylated spirits along the glue line, and replaced with new pieces made from old matching timber, Fig. 47. They may or may not have dust boards fitted into them, but refix the originals if they have. If the dust boards are supporting the drawers by being extended into the plough in the carcase sides, they will be supported by a lath thick enough to fill up the area of the plough not taken up by the thickness of the dust board, and in thickness these will extend at least 1in out from the carcase sides, so that it helps to support the drawer above. It also acts as a kicker for the drawer below to stop it tipping down when the drawer is open.

An alternative to the lath under the dust board was to fit short pieces into the plough with the grain running the same way as the dust board, and covering the same area of the dust board as

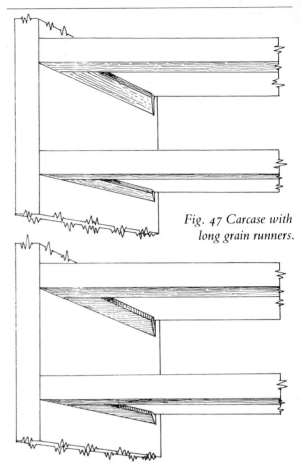

Fig. 47 Carcase with long grain runners.

Fig. 48 Carcase with short grain packings.

that covered when using the lath. This method is by far the strongest and it also allows for any shrinkage of the carcase ends and dust boards because the fillings will shrink at the same time, Fig. 48.

To restore the worn areas of the dust boards, first turn the cabinet upside down, remove the back, and run methylated spirits along the glue lines of the dust board packings, or kickers. It will then be possible to ease them out, working from the back with a strong narrow chisel in the plough, and at the same time dividing the dust board from the kicker with a thin-bladed knife, Fig. 49. Normally these packings extend at least $\frac{1}{2}$in beyond the worn area of the dust board and can be cleaned and used again, but if they do not, new ones will have to be made. A temporary dry lath should be fitted in to replace the kickers.

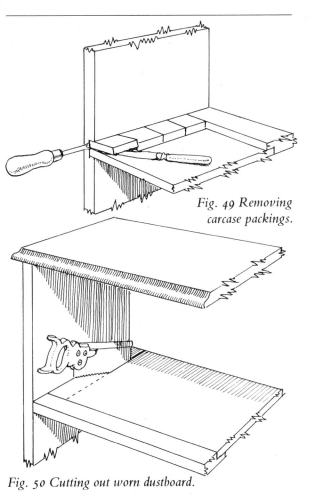

Fig. 49 Removing
carcase packings.

Fig. 50 Cutting out worn dustboard.

For the next operation the carcase must be reversed so that the top is uppermost. Squaring from the front edge of the drawer rail mark a line just clear of the worn area of the dust board from front to back, and using a fine dovetail saw, cut along this line starting at the back until about halfway across. Then the supporting lath can be removed and replaced at the back edge with one of the kickers which will support the back edge of the dust board and also leave clearance for the saw while cutting the rest of the dust board free, Fig. 50.

When both edges of the dust board are cut, check whether the drawer rail has been loosened or forced forward by shrinkage. If it has, tap it forward until half its width protrudes. Re-glue that half of the joint which shows on the rail and the part of the carcase plough into which the rail

fits, and tap the rail back into its correct position. It is better not to remove the rail completely because of damaging the dust board. A piece or pieces should now be fitted to replace the worn area, preferably with the grain running the same way as the dust board grain. They should be glued on both ends and edges when fixing and the short grain packings should be glued to the underside of the dust board, to the new pieces and into the plough at the same time.

MOULDINGS

The restoration of missing cross-band moulding, and moulded cross-band facings will apply mainly to walnut period furniture, but is seen occasionally in other periods.

First measure carefully the width and thickness of the mould to be replaced and the length needed. From a board, approximately 4in wide, cut a piece which is large enough to make up the moulding required. Allow for saw cuts when cutting widths, and also a little extra for finally dressing the edges. Cut or dress the board down to approximately $\frac{1}{16}$in thicker than the net thickness of the mould, and saw off the strips of cross-band a little over the net width of the mould. The cross-banding should now be fitted and glued on to the edge of a pine board which is the same size in thickness as the width of the mould. When the glue has set, the cross-band can be dressed down level to the faces of the pine board and the moulding shape worked on it with a scratch-stock not with moulding planes, because they would tear out the grain. The cross-banding can now be sawn off the pine board, leaving a thin veneer of the pine on the back face to stop it breaking up when cutting and fitting it.

When making a scratch-stock cutter for working a mould, it should be fitted over the original mould at an angle of 85 degrees, not vertical because this is the angle it will be when it is cutting the mould. Cross-banding should never be cut from boards wider than 4in because face shrinkage will cause pull at the outside edges and lifting at the joints. The shorter it is in length the more likely it is to stay firmly fixed.

REMOVING SCREWS AND NAILS

This operation will often prove difficult. Preparation to ease them should be done before attempting to take them out. Apply heat to the head of the screw with a hot soldering iron, the point of an electric clothes iron or a fine-jet blow-torch. If a torch is used, a piece of sheet steel with a hole slightly less than the size of the screw head should be laid over it to avoid the flame spreading and burning the wood. The heat will expand the metal of the screw, and when it has cooled again and contracted it should be less tight in its socket. It also helps to release rust which usually makes the screw tighter. The screwdriver blade should be as wide as possible but within the circumference of the screw head, and should fit snugly into the slot. Any side play in the slot will make the screwdriver more likely to slip out when it is turned, and as the slots are more or less standardised according to the gauge of the screws, it will pay to adjust the blade to a close fit. Before attempting to release the screw by turning anti-clockwise, first try turning it clockwise. It will often move in this direction more easily, and once it has moved should screw out without much trouble. A long screwdriver always gives more leverage than a short one because of the greater torque.

Sometimes the slots of the screws are too shallow for the screwdriver to grip firmly. These can be cut deeper by shaping the point of a large bradawl similar to a screwdriver, and by laying it in the centre of the slot at an angle of approximately 45 degrees and then tapping with a mallet it will cut away shavings of metal until a suitable depth is obtained.

When half the head is missing from a screw it can sometimes be released by putting the point of a punch to the side of the slot and close to the outside circumference of the screw head, and tapping it round gradually with a hammer until the head is high enough to grip with pliers, but more often than not doing this will break off the other half of the head, leaving just the shank. If only the shank of the screw is left, this can be removed by boring round it with a brace and shell-bit, Fig. 51. The gouge-shape of the shell-bit

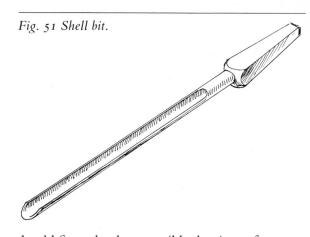

Fig. 51 Shell bit.

should fit as closely as possible the circumference of the screw shank.

When removing nails, the same heat treatment can be used as that used for screws and because old nails usually have a certain amount of taper in their shanks, they can be withdrawn fairly easily. Check that the nails have not been driven right through the wood and clinched on the back (bent over flat to the wood). If they have, then they should be straightened and tapped out until the head can be gripped with pincers. It is advisable to put a piece of metal or strong card under the pincers to lever on. If the nails have not penetrated through to the back, trim a little wood away around the head of the nail so that the points of a pair of nosed side-cutting pliers, Fig. 22, will go under it. With a piece of sheet steel laid under the head of the pliers, lever the nail out until it can be gripped with pincers. If nails protruding through the back are fairly long, it is best to cut them off, so that only about $\frac{1}{8}$in is showing, otherwise they only bend again as they are being driven out. If all these methods fail, the nails can be bored out with a brace and shell-bit, Fig. 51. The hole can be filled by gluing a plug of wood into it.

WARPED OR TWISTED DOORS

These may be corrected by laying the door face down on pads on a bench, and with a fine dovetail saw, cut at the shoulder (where the rail meets the style) to the depth of the tenon at the two high points of the twist of the frame, being careful not

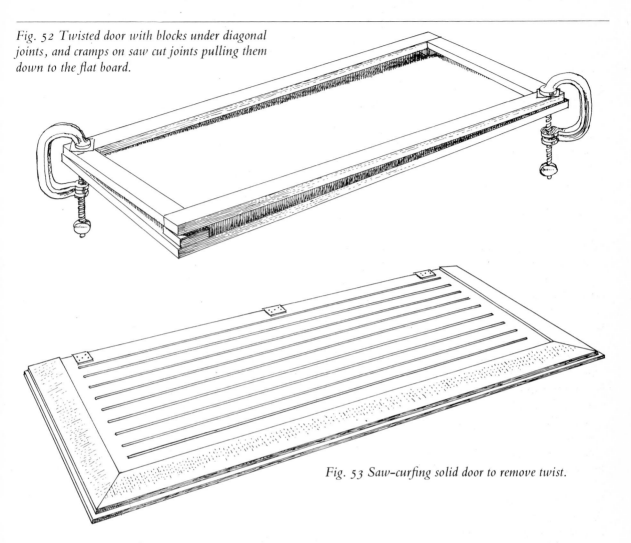

Fig. 52 Twisted door with blocks under diagonal joints, and cramps on saw cut joints pulling them down to the flat board.

Fig. 53 Saw-curfing solid door to remove twist.

to cut into and weaken the tenon. Now lay the door on a thick, flat board such as 1in blockboard approximately the same size as the door, and press one of the high corners down to the board, measure under the other one to find the amount of twist. Divide the measurement by three, and make two blocks to this measurement in thickness and approximately the width of the style. Place the blocks under the low corners of the door. Now feed glue into the two shoulders which have been opened up with the saw and cramp these two corners down until they touch the board, Fig. 52. The shoulders should now be closed up again. Check the shoulders of the two corners with blocks under them and these will probably be open. If they are, a skiver of wood should be fitted into them. Leave the door

cramped to the board until the glue has had time to set. Then release it and leave it for 24 hours before checking it to see whether it is clear of twist. If it is not, repeat the operation on the front of the door.

To remove twist on solid doors, bureau falls, and card table flap-tops, etc., first remove the veneer from the back of the door if any (see page 71) or if a card table or bureau fall remove the felt or baize. A series of saw curfs about 1in apart and in depth three-quarters of the thickness of the door, should now be cut in the back face of the door, Fig. 53. Run it over a circular saw or use a flooring saw with a curved blade as used for taking up floorboards. The curfs should run the same way as the grain and should finish at a convenient distance from the ends, for example, on a card table or bureau fall, up to the cross-band. It should now be laid face down on a flat board and twisted one third the reverse way as described above for panelled doors. The saw curfs should be glued and filled with wood skivers, and left until the glue has set. It can then be dressed and levelled and the veneer or felt refixed to cover up the skivers.

If a solid door or panel is hollow or round on the face but not twisted, it should be saw curfed in the same way as for twist, but if it is round on the face it should have blocks of three to one ratio fitted under each corner, and cramps at the centre of each end to pull it down on the flat board. If it is hollow two blocks would be fitted under the centre at the ends and four cramps used to pull

down the corners. The same procedure would then be followed as that described above for a twisted door. If there are any areas of the saw curfs which cannot be filled with the skivers, such as the ends of the saw curfs which run out at the cross-bands, they should be filled with plaster of Paris and glue size (see page 84). They should never be left open.

Although there are other methods of removing warp or twist in doors, etc., such as putting them in tension the reverse way to the twist, or counter-veneering (veneering on the reverse side to give a counter-pull), the methods described here have proved to be the most reliable. The effect is similar to laminating which has been used in England from early in the 18th century to counter the potential twist in panels.

Leg patterns and carved sculpture

A furniture restorer must be capable of making new legs, because it is often found that the originals have been removed either to reduce a cabinet in height, or more likely because they had been weakened by worm and consequently broken.

In addition, pilaster figures, etc., are often missing and have to be restored. These have often been taken off a cabinet and used for other purposes. These are restored, not with the intention of deceiving, but just to make the cabinet complete, and customers should be informed of what had been done.

Fig. 56 Examples of shaped and carved work.
a *partly completed spiral-twist turning showing the three stages of developing the shape;* **b** *ball and claw foot cabriole leg;* **c** *pad foot cabriole leg;* **d** *scroll foot cabriole leg;* **e** *lion paw foot cabriole leg;* **f** *cherubic figure roughly shaped ready for final carving;* **g** *lathe-turned pad foot cabriole leg.*

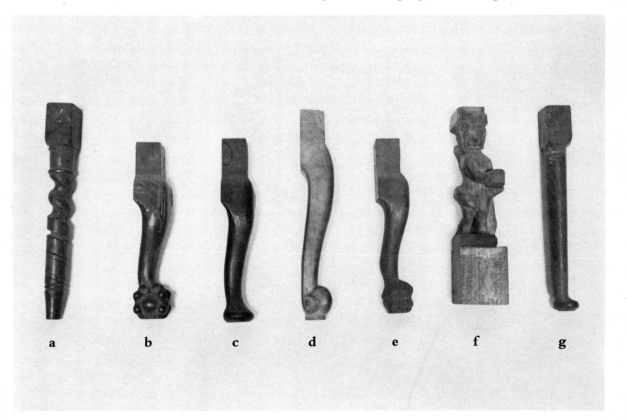

a   b   c   d   e   f   g

Fig. 54 Examples of carving chisels.

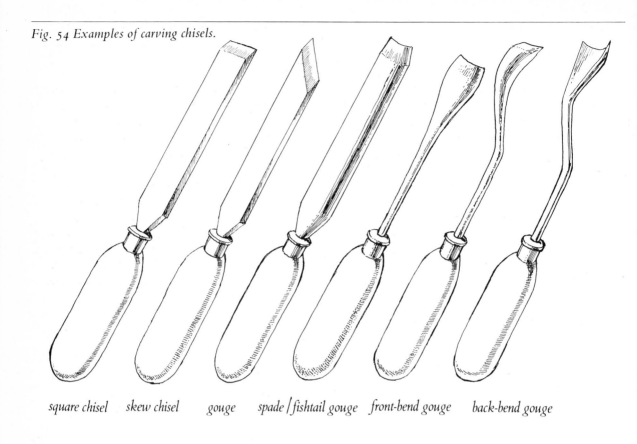

square chisel   skew chisel   gouge   spade / fishtail gouge   front-bend gouge   back-bend gouge

Fig. 55 Examples of carving tools and mallet.

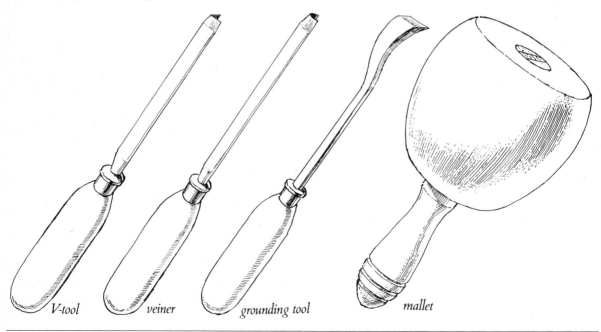

V-tool   veiner   grounding tool   mallet

CABRIOLE LEGS

For cabriole legs to be correct in shape and proportions there are certain rules which should be followed when making patterns for them. Unfortunately, these rules were not always adhered to by the old carvers and furniture makers, particularly those working in the rural areas. However, it is necessary for the restorer to know these rules even though they may have to be ignored when matching up an original leg.

The pad foot cabriole

First cut and square up the timber to exact width and thickness but leaving a little extra in the length. Make the worst two adjoining faces the face side and the face edge, because they will be the faces on which the rails will be jointed but they will also be the back of the leg, then square one end.

Make a cardboard pattern which fits exactly the width of the face side and edge of the timber and mark out the shape as shown in Fig. 57. Note area of timber running through from top to bottom of leg. This should not be less than $\frac{1}{4}$in in width. With a sharp veneer knife, cut out the pattern accurately to shape, cutting on the solid lines at the foot, not on the dotted lines. Lay the pattern on the face side of the timber with its back edge tight up to the face edge and mark out the outline. Then lay the pattern on the face edge with its back edge tight up to the face side and mark that out. When marking these faces make

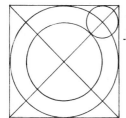

setting-out bottom square of leg,
for final shape of foot

Fig. 57 Patterns for pad foot cabriole leg.

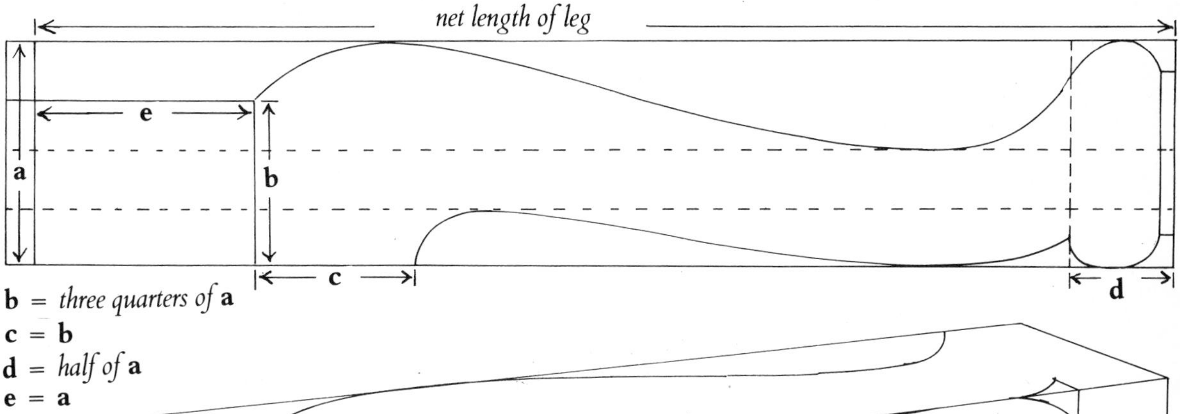

net length of leg

a

b

e

c

d

b = *three quarters of* **a**
c = **b**
d = *half of* **a**
e = **a**

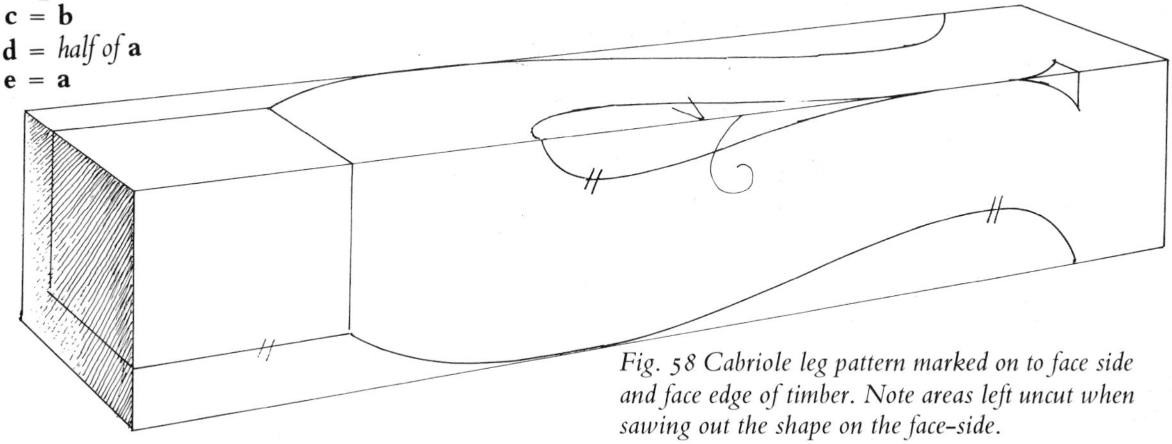

Fig. 58 Cabriole leg pattern marked on to face side and face edge of timber. Note areas left uncut when sawing out the shape on the face-side.

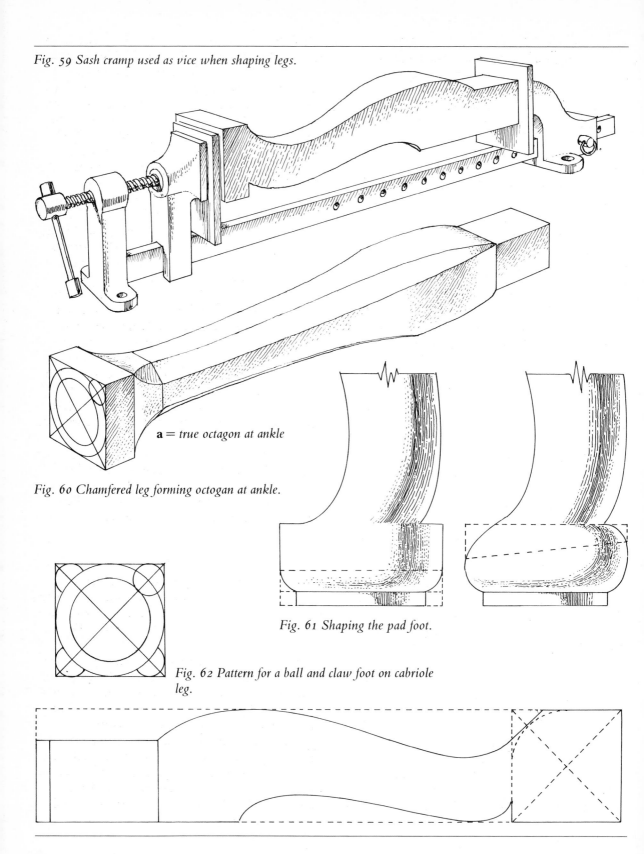

Fig. 59 Sash cramp used as vice when shaping legs.

a = *true octagon at ankle*

Fig. 60 Chamfered leg forming octogan at ankle.

Fig. 61 Shaping the pad foot.

Fig. 62 Pattern for a ball and claw foot on cabriole
    leg.

sure, of course, that the bottom edge of the pattern is tight up to the squared end of the timber, Fig. 58.

To mark out the bottom of the feet, first strike diagonal lines across to find the centre, then with a compass point at the centre, strike a circle which touches the outside faces of the square. With the compass point on a position where the first circle cuts a diagonal line, strike a second circle which touches two of the outside faces, and with the point of the compass back in the centre of the square strike a third circle with its circumference just touching the circumference of the small circle. The first circle is the overall size of the foot, and the third circle is the size of the pad under the foot, Fig. 57.

With a bow saw or a band saw, the pattern shape on the face side can now be cut, making sure that the saw blade is cutting truely at right-angles to the face side, and close up to the outside edge of the lines. The pieces should not be cut off completely or the lines will be lost for cutting the face edge. Leave approximately $\frac{1}{8}$in uncut at an area where the saw is cutting with the grain, Fig. 58. The face edge shape can now be cut out, and when that is completed, the pieces left on from cutting the face side can be broken loose and removed.

To check that the sawing is accurate, cast your eye along the length of the front angle of the legs and along the length of the back angle of the legs. Both should appear as a straight line. If they do not, they should be adjusted by dressing off the high point on the appropriate face with a spoke-shave. A sash cramp fixed to the bench is the best vice to use when shaping legs, Fig. 59.

With a round-faced spokeshave, which will fit into the sharp curve of the foot, chamfer off the angles at the ankle of the legs until the section through the ankle forms a true octagon. Work the chamfers up the length of the leg, parallel in width to those at the ankle, until they curve back, then taper them off to a point, Fig. 60. The angles on the leg are now rounded off until the ankle section is a true circle and the other parts are rounded evenly into the flat areas.

To form the pad foot, strike out the circles as shown, Fig. 57, and with a carver's V-tool make a cut round the perimeter of the inner circle, $\frac{1}{8}$in in depth. With a coping saw or chisel trim off the the corners of the square section to the line of the outer circle. With a spokeshave and gouge trim off the lower section of the foot until it is level to the depth of the V-cut and is a true quarter-round. With rasp and file or carving chisels, round over the top back edge of the foot so forming half of a circle over approximately one third of the circumference of the foot; at the same time trimming off the lower part of the leg until it shapes smoothly into the ankle. With the front centre of the foot uppermost in the vice, and with a spokeshave cutting at an angle of 45 degrees, round over half of the foot at a time, starting a little before the centre of the toe and cutting until it shapes smoothly into the ankle. When both halves of the front of the foot are shaped, the front of the toe should be a little lower than the heel, Fig. 61. If a lathe is available the rounding and shaping of the foot can be worked on it, but the final shaping at the ankle and front of the toe will still have to be done with a spokeshave, rasp or file.

The final cleaning-up of the leg surface is best done with a square-edge comma-scraper, Fig. 18, but the area at the knee should be left until the wings are glued in position and dressed and levelled.

The ball and claw cabriole leg

The details of working the leg part of all cabriole legs is virtually the same as described for the pad foot cabriole, but the ball and claw foot is formed from a full cube of the timber, Fig. 62.

After cutting out the leg to the pattern, work the leg to the final shape from the ankle to the knee, and mark out the underside of the foot as shown in Fig. 62. With a carver's V-tool cut round the perimeter of the inner circle to a depth of approximately $\frac{1}{8}$in to form the pad under the foot. With the same tool make cuts on each side of the small circles in the corners to the depth of the large circle, which is the size of the ball, and parallel to the side of the cube to its overall height, Fig. 63.

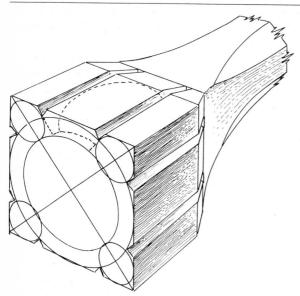

Fig. 63 Cuts in angle at side of claws on ball and claw foot.

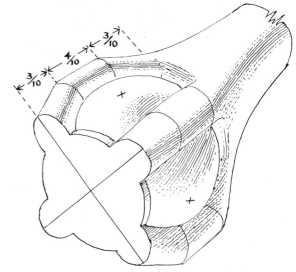

Fig. 64 Ball shape and claw angles formed.

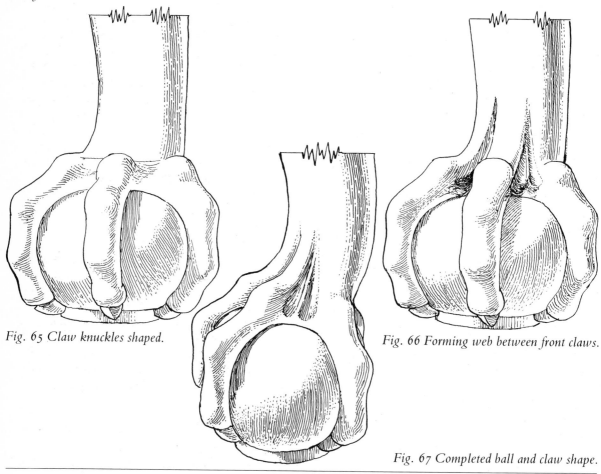

Fig. 65 Claw knuckles shaped.

Fig. 66 Forming web between front claws.

Fig. 67 Completed ball and claw shape.

Mark the centres on all four sides of the cube, and with a carver's fishtail gouge, which fits accurately the circumference of the large circle and which is approximately a third of the width of the cube, carve away the surplus timber to form the sphere for the ball between the claws. Make certain that the centre mark is not cut away, and then shape into the pad at the bottom end and a similar distance over the top end.

Select a back-bend spade carving gouge which fits accurately the circumference of the claw circles and work the face of the claws into a half-round. Measuring from the base of the foot, mark three tenths of the height of the cube on all four claws, and from these points mark off four tenths of the height of the foot (or measuring from the base of the foot seven tenths). With the same back-bend gouge, pare back the upper and lower section of the three front claws to the points marked at an angle of 45 degrees, Fig. 64, and on the back claw pare off the lower end only. With the back-bend gouge, work a spherical shape on the three high angle points of the three front claws to form the knuckles, and on the back claw the two lower angles only, at the same time hollow out the area between the claw knuckles by reversing the gouge, round face down, and paring until three quarters of the overall thickness of the claw is left in the lowest point of the hollow. The lowest point on the centre hollows of the three front claws should finish up exactly in line with the high points of the ball sphere, Fig. 65.

To remove the surplus timber at the top end of the ball between the front claws take a carver's front-bend gouge with a circumference the same as that used for the claws and with the low point of the cutting edge touching the sphere of the ball and the side cutting edge first to the side of the right knuckle and then to the side of the left knuckle, cut out a quarter circle which rises from the face of the ball and tapers out to nothing just below the ankle and central on the leg at that point. This will produce a high point central between the claws, Fig. 66.

With the back-bend gouge used for the claws now pare off the surplus timber at the top of the claws, tapering them away to nil at the ankle. Then using a straight gouge, which fits the circumference of the inner circle under the foot, trim off the front edge of the web between the claws, shaping from close up to the claws and from the hollow under the top knuckles. With the same gouge lying on the side of the bottom knuckle with the cutting edge facing the claw nails, and cutting at an angle of about 45 degrees, trim off the claw nails to form a high point on the front centre and tapered to the pad, leaving them about $\frac{1}{16}$in wide at their lowest point. Also bevel the top end of the claw nails at an angle of 45 degrees into the bottom knuckle.

Using the same gouge, work a hollow above the knuckle of the back claw and under the ankle, curving downwards so that it shapes the top end of the claw and finishing with a curve on the top end of the ball. Now shape the ankle into this curve. Cutting into the face of the ball about $\frac{1}{32}$in trim back the upper part of the ball to this level with the spade gouge which was used to shape the ball, thus giving the impression that the ball is being squeezed by the weight on top of it. With the back-bend claw gouge, shape the upper part of the claw into the hollow of the curve, Fig. 67. Finally undercut the claws with the ball gouge about $\frac{1}{32}$in from the ball and at an angle of 45 degrees. The foot is now ready for cleaning and finishing with the square-edged, comma-shaped scraper.

The scroll-foot cabriole leg
Square up the timber and make the worst adjoining sides the face side and face edge and then square one end. A card pattern is made the same shape as that for a ball and claw leg, because the scroll foot is also formed out of a cube of the timber size. Mark out the timber as shown in Fig. 62 and work leg to octagon shape (see pad foot pattern, Fig. 60). The front and rear faces of the leg angles can now be rounded over, but the angle at the sides faces should be left square, Fig. 68.

On the underside of the foot line, across from the diagonal corners and from the point where they cross, place the point of the compass and

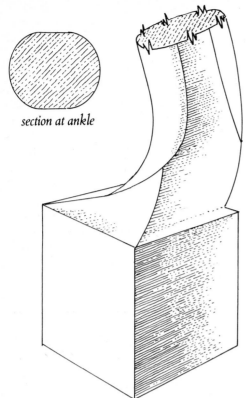

section at ankle

Fig. 68 Shaping leg of scroll foot cabriole.

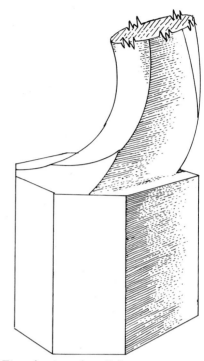

Fig. 70 First shaping of scroll foot.

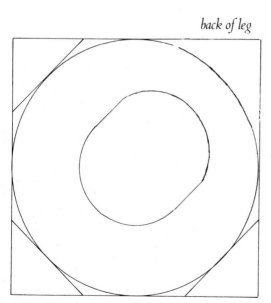

back of leg

Fig. 69 Marking out base of scroll foot.

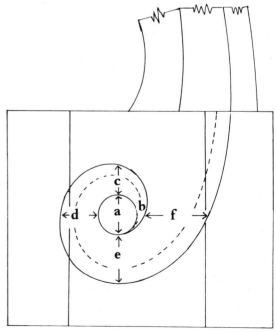

Fig. 71 Marking out scroll shape.

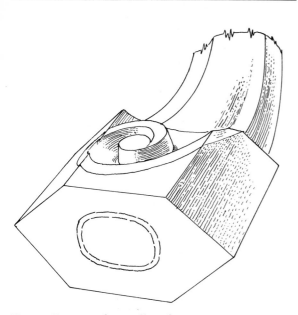

Fig. 72 First cuts for scroll on foot.

strike a circle which touches the four sides of the square of the timber. With the compass on the same centre strike a second circle with a radius one fifth the width of the cube. For example, if the cube sides measure $2\frac{1}{2}$in, the radius of the circle will be $\frac{1}{2}$in. From the point where the small circle crosses the diagonal which runs from the centre to the back of the leg, strike a second circle the same size, and join the circumferences of the two circles together with straight lines. This is the correct shape for the pad under the scroll foot. At each angle of the leg square strike a line at 45 degrees which just touches the circumference of the large circle, thus forming an octagon, Fig. 69. Remove the timber on the front and two side faces to form the octagon shape but leaving the back one complete, Fig. 70. With a carver's V-tool cut round the outline of the pad shape under the foot to a depth of $\frac{1}{8}$in.

On the two square faces of the octagon which form the sides of the foot, mark off half the height of the cube and strike a circle in the centre of each, with a diameter equalling one fifth of the height of the cube. Mark out the scroll shape as in Fig. 71; if in ratio $\mathbf{a} = 4$, then $\mathbf{b} = 1$, $\mathbf{c} = 2$,

$\mathbf{d} = 3$, $\mathbf{e} = 4$ and $\mathbf{f} = 5$. With a carving chisel which fits accurately the circumference of circle $\mathbf{a}$ and in width is approximately one third of the circumference, hold the chisel in a vertical position from the side face, and with one point of the cutting edge at position $\mathbf{b}$ cut round the upper half of the circumference to a depth of $\frac{1}{8}$in, continuing until position $\mathbf{e}$ is reached. Take a chisel which fits the circumference from $\mathbf{e}$ to $\mathbf{c}$ and repeat the operation until a position about halfway between $\mathbf{c}$ and $\mathbf{d}$ is reached. Take a chisel which fits the circumference $\mathbf{d}$ to $\mathbf{e}$ and continue the cutting to $\mathbf{e}$. With a chisel which fits $\mathbf{e}$ to $\mathbf{f}$ cut until $\mathbf{f}$ is reached. Take a No. 3 three-quarter inch carving chisel held at right-angles to the face of the surface now being cut and continue the scroll cut to the top of the cube.

With a No. 5 three-quarter inch carving chisel held so that it cuts parallel to the surface $\mathbf{a}$, cut away the surplus timber starting with nil at $\mathbf{b}$ and paring and increasing depth gradually until at $\mathbf{e}$ it is equal in depth to one fifth of the cube, from $\mathbf{e}$ to $\mathbf{f}$ should be cut parallel to surface $\mathbf{a}$. Care should be taken not to lose the original scroll shape vertical cut by increasing its depth as required.

On the new surface mark out a second scroll line with the ratio $\mathbf{a} = 4$ as before but with $\mathbf{c} = 1$, $\mathbf{d} = 2$, $\mathbf{e} = 3$, $\mathbf{f} = 4$. With the carving chisels used in the same rotation as used for cutting the original outline of the scroll, but with them laid at an angle of approximately 30 degrees off the face of $\mathbf{a}$, cut from nil at $\mathbf{b}$ to one at $\mathbf{c}$ and so on until $\mathbf{f}$ is reached and the bevel should then be gradually adjusted until it levels up with the face of the leg at the ankle, Fig. 72. Repeat the operation on the reverse side of the foot. With the carving chisel which was used for vertically cutting the original scroll shape at position $\mathbf{b}$ cut a double ogee shape on the front of the cube with the round touching the front face of the octagon and the ends of the ogee on the line of the original scroll. Now cut the hollows round the underside of the foot following the shape of the scroll and cutting back to the $\frac{1}{8}$in depth at the sides of the pad; round and complete the ogee shape up to the pad. On the back underside of the foot work the ogee shape but with the hollows

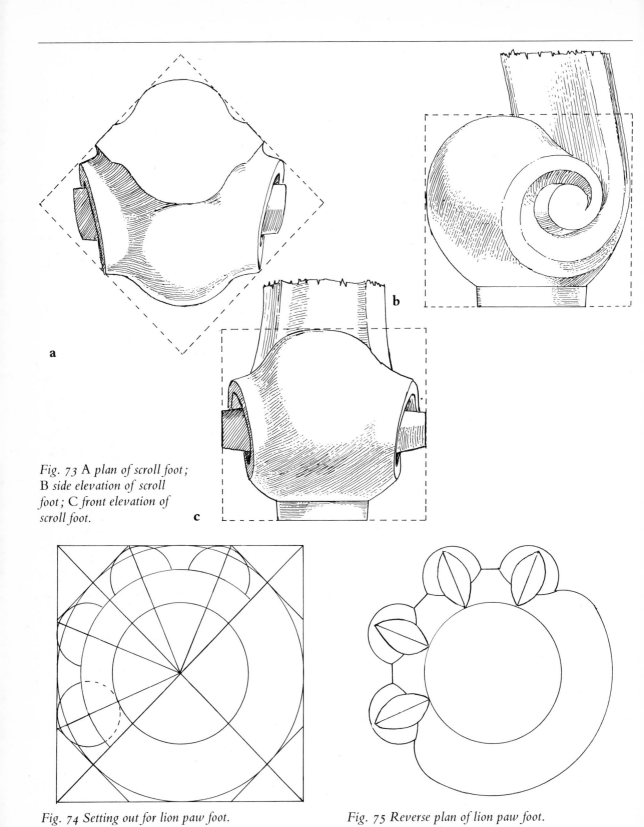

Fig. 73 A plan of scroll foot; B side elevation of scroll foot; C front elevation of scroll foot.

a

b

c

Fig. 74 Setting out for lion paw foot.

Fig. 75 Reverse plan of lion paw foot.

tapering out to nil at **f**. Repeat the operation on the front top of the foot with the outside edge of the ogee following the shape of the scroll and the high point of the round touching the top edge of the cube. The front and back faces of the legs can now be pared down until they shape neatly into the foot ogee, see Fig. 73.

The leg is now ready for cleaning up with the comma scraper. When finally cleaning up with garnet paper, glass paper, etc, the surfaces should be damped down with water at least once to raise the grain.

Although there are a number of variations in the shapes of scroll feet, providing the marking out is copied so that it matches the shape required, there should be no difficulty if these general instructions are carefully followed, but when copying an original leg, it is important that the carving chisels should be fitted to it to make sure they are the right size and shape. It is most important that there is no variation in the curves as only a small difference will alter the final shape of the leg considerably.

Lion paw foot

The instructions for making the card pattern for the lion paw leg are the same as those for a ball and claw leg; the foot is formed from a cube and the leg from the ankle upwards is the same shape as the pad foot, Fig. 60. After squaring up and cutting out the leg shape, strike out an octagon on the underside of the foot using the full size of the square, and then strike a line from the centre point to the octagon angles which form the two front faces of the foot. Now strike a half-circle four-fifths of the size of the square on the front half of the foot and with the point of the compass where the lines to the angles cut this circle, strike four half-circles which touch the lines of the octagon. By completing one of these circles the position of the pad under the foot is found, Fig. 74. The surplus timber at the angles of the square can now be removed to form the octagon shape, and a carver's V-tool is used to remove the surplus timber on each side of the four claws. To shape the claws and the claw nails follow the instructions for the ball and claw foot. With the carver's V-tool cut round the outline

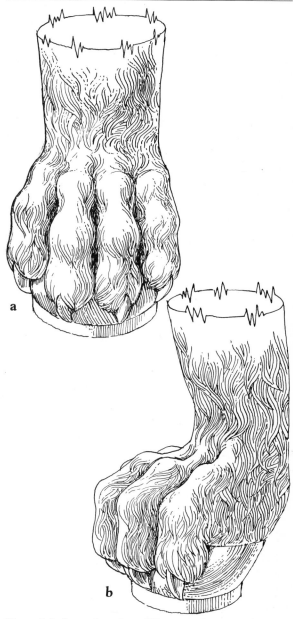

Fig. 76 A *front elevation of lion paw foot*; B *side elevation of lion paw foot*.

of the circle of the pad to a depth of $\frac{1}{8}$in before shaping the claw nails.

The ball shape on the rear of the foot can now be shaped using a chisel which fits accurately the outer circle of the setting out. The rear section of the ball will be accurate to the shape of the chisel but will be tapered away at the sides to the low

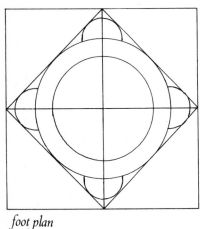

foot plan

Fig. 77 Setting out for front-facing ball and claw cabriole leg.

Fig. 78 A side elevation pattern for front-facing cabriole leg; B front elevation pattern for front-facing cabriole leg.

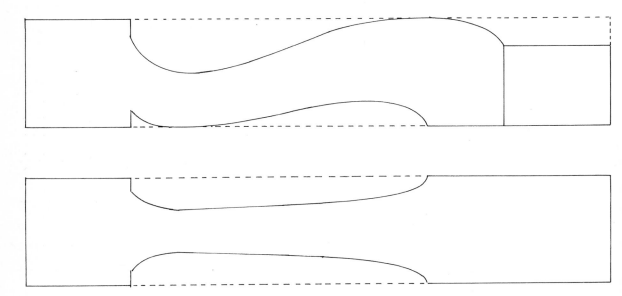

point at the sides of the claws, Fig. 75. The foot is now ready for the simulated hair and this is done with a carver's small veining tool by a series of short cuts running lengthway on the claws and leg, not across them, and finishing in a point at the back of the ankle, Fig. 76.

Front-facing cabriole leg
The pattern for making a front-facing ball and claw cabriole leg is similar to that for a corner leg, but if the size of the foot has to match in size a corner leg, then it is necessary for the square of the timber to be increased by half as much again. For example, if the corner leg is made out of 2in square timber, then a front-facing leg must be 3in

square to allow for the claws, which on the corner legs are worked in the angle, Fig. 77. In addition, a second pattern is needed for the front face shape and this must match the side pattern for ankle size, Fig. 78. Other types of cabriole legs such as the lion paw, scroll and pad foot, are worked out of an octagon shape which does not require the extra timber size, but they do, of course, require the face and side patterns.

Splay-leg cabrioles
Two patterns are required for the splay-leg cabrioles, one for the side elevation and one for the front face; Fig. 79 shows the front and side patterns for a ball and claw foot. It is not neces-

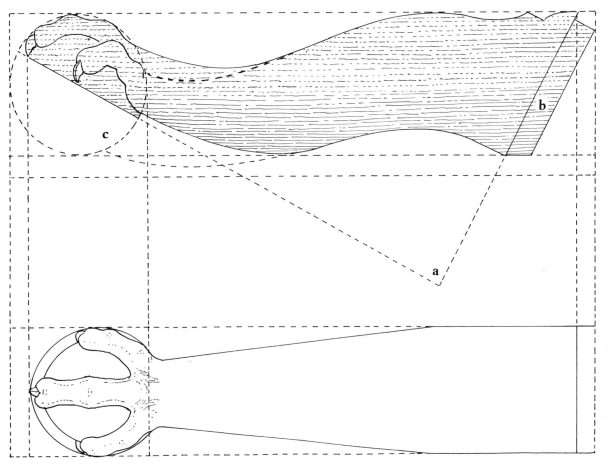

Fig. 79 Patterns for splay ball and claw cabriole leg.

sary, of course, to show the claws on the pattern, only the segment circle outlines. There are various features which should be specially noted.

1. The leg can be adjusted in height by moving position point **a** but it must always be a right-angle and the base line must always pass through the centre of the circle at the foot, with the exception of the scroll foot, when it should touch the lowest point of the circumference of the circle.

2. The size of the timber must be accurate to the rectangular dash outline on both the side pattern and the front pattern.

3. Note the shortening off of the front face pattern for the ball and claw foot because of the angle of the foot on the side pattern. This shortening would also apply to the pad and lion paw feet, the exception would be the scroll foot which would line up with the front of the circumference of the circle.

4. The position of the ankle is also changed on the scroll foot **c** and this will probably necessitate increasing the width of the timber.

5. Do not forget to allow the timber for joint **b**.

6. The back face of the scroll leg is usually left

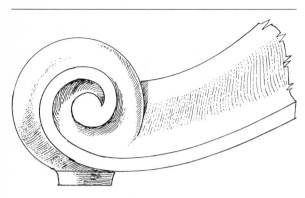

Fig. 80 Side elevation for scroll splay foot.

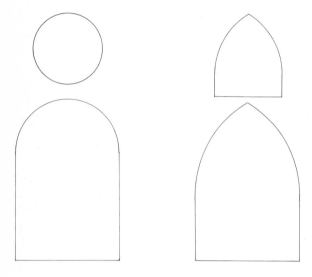

Fig. 81 Reverse plan of pad foot, and ankle shape of splay cabriole.

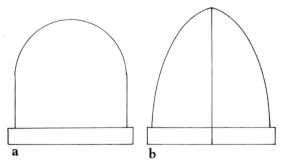

a   b

Fig. 82 Front view section of pad feet or splay cabriole.

flat, and the front face shaped in a double ogee to match the foot, Fig. 80 similar to that on the straight leg, Fig. 73A.

Pad feet plans for alternative foot shapes, and also the ankle section, are shown in Fig. 81. The side elevation pattern would be the same as that shown for the ball and claw feet, the front face pattern would have the shape of the foot changed, but the width of the foot would remain the same.

To shape the legs of the splay-leg cabrioles follow the same procedure as that for straight-leg cabrioles. The leg shape for pad foot shown in Fig. 82 A would, of course, have a flat back face and the point on the front of the leg usually runs up the full length of the leg. Pad foot, Fig. 82 B, is shaped in the same way as a straight leg. Fig. 82 shows the front sections of the two feet, the extended pad at the base of the foot may be omitted if desired.

The lathe-turned cabriole leg

When making the pattern for these legs the foot is shaped out of half the cube height of the timber, and at cube or ankle height the leg is two-thirds of the thickness of the timber. For the legs to be accurate in shape both the pattern and the timber must be the correct length, Fig. 83. With the lathe centres set in **a** and **b** turn the leg from below the top square in a parallel round over the rest of its length, and at the full thickness of the timber, and then shape the foot as shown in Fig. 84. For the second operation, Fig. 85, keep the lathe centre in position **a** but move the centre at the foot into position **c** and set to two-thirds of the thickness of the timber with calipers. Turn and gauge the ankle to size, at the same time rounding off into the foot. The surplus timber can now be removed from above the ankle to the underside of the square. The turning is now complete but it is usually necessary to trim at the heel with a rasp or file.

If the legs are going to be fixed at the corners of a frame then the lathe centre will be fitted in position **d**, Fig. 86, on the diagonal, but if the leg needs to be front facing, as required for a round or oval frame, then the lathe centre will be fitted in position **e** central on line **c**.

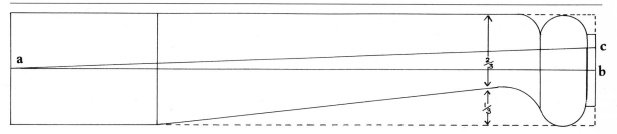

Fig. 83 Pattern for lathe-turned cabriole leg.

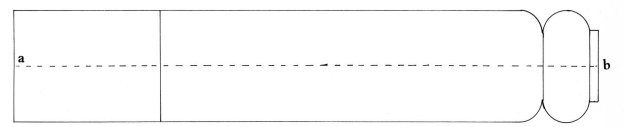

Fig. 84

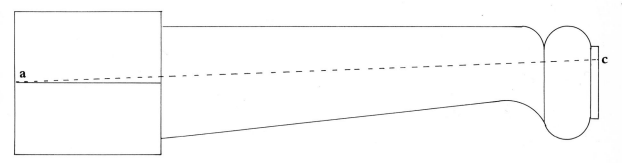

Fig. 85

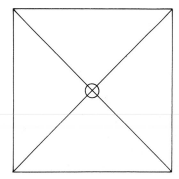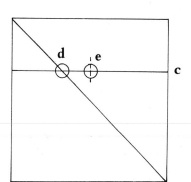

Fig. 86 Lathe centre positions for turned cabriole leg.

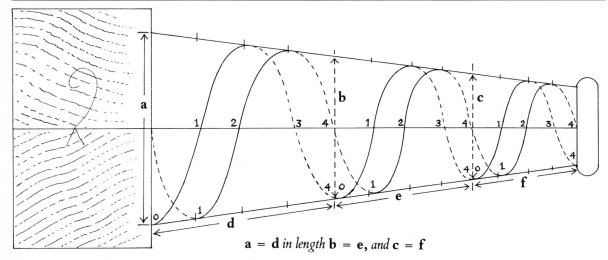

$a = d$ *in length* $b = e,$ *and* $c = f$

Fig. 87 Pattern for spiral twist turning.

The spiral-twist turning

The spiral-twist leg pattern, Fig. 87, is shown
with an exaggerated taper in order to demon-
strate the reduction of the height of the twist
according to the width of the taper. Mark a face
side and a face edge on the top square of the
timber, or in a position where it will not be
removed when turning it in the lathe. Centre the
two ends and fit it into the lathe with the end
intended for the square at the headstock and turn
to the shape and taper required. With compasses
set at one-quarter of the width of the turning at
a, **b**, or **c**, according to the section being worked
on, mark off positions **1** and **2** in line with the
diagonal of the face side and edge of the top
square, spin to the next diagonal and mark
positions **3** and **4**, spin to the next diagonal and
mark at positions **1** and **4**, the points can now be
joined together with a pencil line in numerical
order as shown on the pattern, starting at **0** for
the two separate spirals.

Using the lathe as a holding jig, with a coping
saw or similar (not a dovetail saw which would
become buckled because of the twist in the spiral)
start at **1** and cut down to one-fifth of the
thickness of the leg along the pencil line, taper
out the cut to nil at **0**. Then cut round the rest of
the spiral at a depth of one-fifth until position **3** is
reached at the bottom of the turning, it should

then be tapered out to nil at position **4**. This
operation should be repeated on the second spiral.
The waste timber between the two spiral cuts can
now be removed with a chisel, to the depth of the
saw cuts, Fig. 88, and the edges chamfered off at
an angle of 45 degrees as shown in Fig. 89. The
shaping can now be done with carving gouges or,
if preferred, with rasps and files, Fig. 90. The
comma-shaped scraper is useful for final cleaning
up of the surfaces. On high quality cabinets, etc,
the spiral-twists run clockwise at the right of the
cabinet and anti-clockwise at the left.

Spiral fluted or reeded turnings

When setting out and preparing either of these
turnings the special holding jig, Fig. 10, page 15,
should be used. After fixing the turning in the
jig and setting the jig straight-edge so that it runs
parallel with the top face of the turning, take a
marking gauge and mark the top centre of the
face over the length of the turning, using the jig
straight-edge as a guide.

With calipers take the width of the turning at the
narrow end and mark this distance from the bead
or quirk down the length of the turning. Hold a
pencil point up to this mark and spin the turning
so that this distance is marked round the circumference of the turning. Reset the calipers to the
diameter of the turning at this mark and lay this

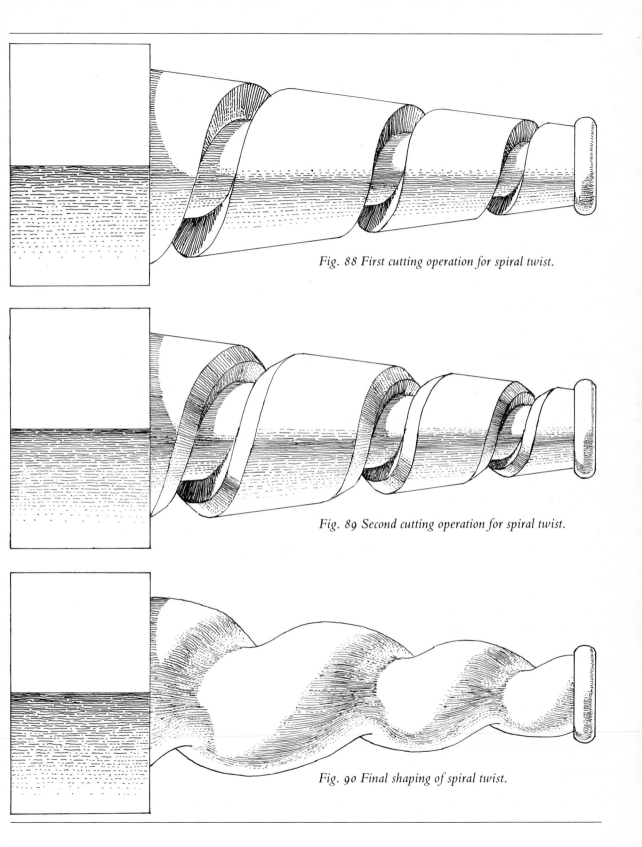

Fig. 88 First cutting operation for spiral twist.

Fig. 89 Second cutting operation for spiral twist.

Fig. 90 Final shaping of spiral twist.

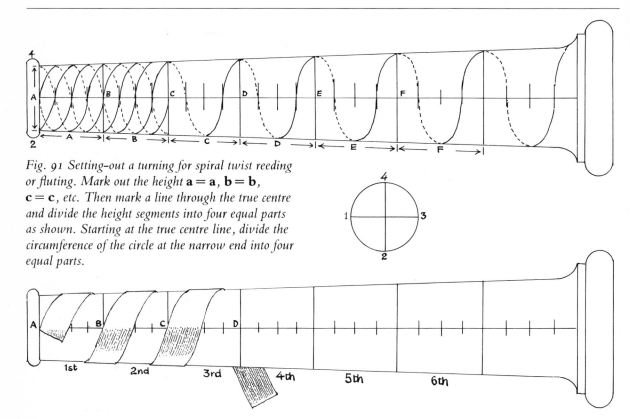

Fig. 91 Setting-out a turning for spiral twist reeding or fluting. Mark out the height **a** = **a**, **b** = **b**, **c** = **c**, etc. Then mark a line through the true centre and divide the height segments into four equal parts as shown. Starting at the true centre line, divide the circumference of the circle at the narrow end into four equal parts.

Fig. 92 Marking out a turning for spiral reeding or fluting.

Using a narrow strip of card or thin pliable plastic, put one point of it at position **a** and spiral it round the turning so that its edge touches the position where the centre line cuts the first height division line, **b**. If this is difficult to hold in position, two drawing pins can be used at positions **a** and **b**, while a line is pencilled on the turning along the edge of the card

from **a** to **b**, repeat the operation from **b** to **c** and **c** to **d** and so on over the length of the turning. With the point of the card now on the 2nd position of the circumference, and its edge passing through the line of the width of the first segment at centre line, finish on the division line directly in line with its starting position. This will line up parallel with the first spiral line, repeat this over the length of the turning. The same procedure is worked from the 3rd and 4th circumference positions.

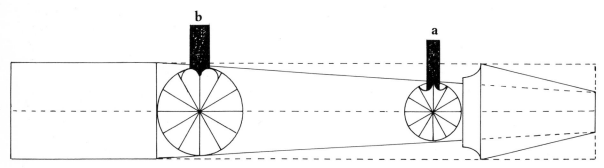

Fig. 93 Pattern for turned leg with straight flutes or reeds.

off down a further section of the turning and repeat this operation over the full length of the turning. Divide each of these sections into equal parts according to the number of flutes required on the turning, which will vary according to the size of its circumference. It should be realised that flutes or reeds in spiral twist take up approximately twice the width on the circumference that a straight flute takes, Fig. 91. The circumference directly under the bead or quirk should be marked off with the same number of divisions as the height sections, Fig. 91 **a** (the example is marked off in four sections).

For marking off the setting out of the rest of the spiral twists follow the instructions on the diagram, Fig. 92.

With a coping saw or similar cut down the spiral lines to a depth of half the width of the flutes at their narrowest end, these cuts are the centres of the flutes or, if reeding, the cuts will be the edges of the reeds. Gouges and files can be used to remove the main part of the surplus wood, but scratch-stock cutters should be used finally to get them clean and even.

Turned, fluted or reeded legs

First make a cardboard pattern of the leg to make sure that the proportions are correct, this can then be used as a marking-off lath when turning. If the leg is going to be fluted, and it is tapered, strike a circle within the smallest end of the taper of the pattern and set out on the circumference the number of flutes required. Make a square-edge cutter which fits over the high point between the flutes and follows the curve of the flute on each side of it to just a fraction over half their width, Fig. 93 **a**.

If the legs are going to be reeded, strike a circle within the largest end which is going to be reeded, and fit a cutter into the low point between the reeds to pass at least halfway over the reed on each side of it, Fig. 93 **b**. The legs can now be turned putting the smallest end, if tapered, to the headstock, and by using the index plate (Fig. 24, page 20) the lathe can be used with the fixing pin as a holding jig when fluting or reeding.

A special straight-edge guide, Fig. 25, page 20, is also required for the scratch-stock, Fig. 11, and this can be made from two blocks which fit firmly on the lathe bed and extend forward about 4in beyond the lathe centres. If they are made of wood bore a hole in the two blocks, $\frac{3}{4}$in from their front edge and central in width, to receive $\frac{1}{2}$in bolts. These should be long enough to reach at least 3in above the lathe centres when the head is sunk into the wood on the underside of the block. If the blocks are metal the bolts can be tapped and threaded into the blocks instead of having a sunken head. The bolts must be threaded over their full length so that a locking nut can be screwed down tightly on to the top of the blocks to hold the head or thread firmly. Two extra nuts with washers are required for each bolt to hold the straight-edge in position. If the straight-edge is made of wood it should be $1\frac{1}{2}$in $\times$ $\frac{3}{4}$in in section with a series of holes, $\frac{9}{16}$in in size, bored in the centre of its $1\frac{1}{2}$in face at intervals of approximately 3in over its entire length. If the straight-edge is made of metal the holes should be $\frac{1}{32}$in over size ($\frac{17}{32}$in). The metal straight-edge is now fitted on to the bolts with its top edge running parallel to the top edge of the taper of the leg, and with the straight-edge of the guide nearest to the operator, parallel to the lathe centres. The cutter is fitted into the scratch-stock where its centre will be immediately over the top centre of the leg when the scratch-stock guide is laying tight up to the straight-edge face. Make sure that the leg is firm between the lathe centres.

The index plate, which will have been previously set up on the lathe, can now be set for the number of flutes or reeds required. For example, if eight are required then the pin is fitted into the index plate at any No. 8 marked on the plate and the scratch-stock is used to work the first two halves of the reeds or flutes. The index pin is then fitted into the next No. 8 on the plate and the scratch-stock operation repeated. This is continued until the circumference of the leg is completely fluted or reeded. It may not be possible to get the ends of the flutes perfect with the scratch-stock but these can easily be completed with carver's gouges. There may also be a thin wafer of wood left in the centre of the widest end of the flutes and this should be removed with a gouge.

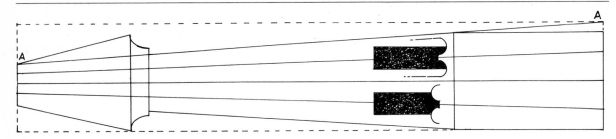

Fig. 94 Pattern for square section reeded or fluted leg.
Note: position a:a is required when working for
fluted legs and can be obtained by laying the pattern
on the leg in the jig, also the flutes are rounded and
tapered-out at the top and bottom ends, which is
easiest done with carver's gouges.

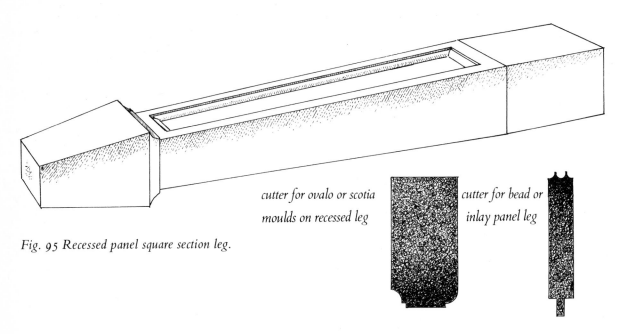

cutter for ovalo or scotia
moulds on recessed leg

cutter for bead or
inlay panel leg

Fig. 95 Recessed panel square section leg.

The special holding jig, Fig. 10, page 15, may be used instead of the lathe by fixing a small ply-wood disc which has been marked out for the number of flutes or reeds required, central on the bottom of the foot with panel pins. With a top centre mark on the jig, the positions can be set in the same way as they are set with the index plate. When using the jig for turned legs, the horizontal rest on each end of the jig is removed so that the leg will spin freely on the centre pins. The horizontal slides must be set central on the jig and the straight-edge set so that the top face of the leg is level and parallel to it.

Square section, parallel or tapered legs can also be fluted or reeded using this special holding jig (Fig. 10, page 15). A pattern of the leg must first be made but before marking out the reeds or flutes, cut out and shape the legs accurately to the size and shape of the pattern. If for any reason the shape of the legs has to be adjusted then the shape of the pattern should also be adjusted to match before setting out the positions of the flutes or reeds. The legs and the pattern should be made accurately to length as well as to width and thickness, otherwise there will be difficulty in getting the position of the fluting or reeding correct.

Next mark out the position of the flutes or reeds and when they have been set out carefully on the pattern, draw a line accurately through the centre of each one and extend it through to the top and bottom edge of the pattern, Fig. 94.

Lay the pattern accurately on each of the four sides of the legs and mark the centre points between the flutes or reeds on to the top and bottom angles of the legs. Lay a leg on the horizontal rests in the jig with the point of the first flute to the centre points marked on the jig and clamp up the jig until the metal points on the slides of the jig grip the leg firmly. The straight-edge guide should now be adjusted until it is level and parallel to the top face of the leg. The scratch-stock guide should be laid tight up to the straight-edge and the centre point of the cutter positioned accurately on the centre point of the jig, the first flute or reed can now be worked. Slacken off the jig and move the leg until the next centres are opposite the centre lines on the jig and repeat the process until all four sides have been moulded.

Sunken–panel legs

These can also be worked in the special holding jig, Fig. 10. The cutters used for recessing the panels should, of course, be square-edged and with the edge which cuts and levels the base of the recess not more than $\frac{1}{2}$in wide if a clean finish is to be obtained. It is usual to remove most of the waste timber in the recess with a chisel or router before using the cutter in the scratch-stock, and the top and bottom edges of the panel will be shaped with gouges and chisels, Fig. 95. The cutter is shaped for both ovolo and scotia edging because the cutter has a cutting edge on either face. The guide on the scratch-stock is kept tight up to the side of the leg, not up to the straight-edge on the jig. The effect of a panelled leg is often achieved by using line inlay, or a flush bead, and this is worked by the same method as that used for the sunken panel but using the scratch-stock cutter, Fig. 95, and if the top and bottom of the leg are squared–up to length the ends of the panels can also be worked with the scratch-stock cutter.

Restoring missing carving

Before commencing to reproduce pieces of carving which are missing, be certain that the surface shape matches the original, this applies particularly to mouldings, the least discrepancy will be exaggerated when the carving is finished. Select the carving chisels required by laying them on the various curves of the original carving and making sure that they fit the circumferences, etc.

MOULDS

The setting out required for ovolo moulds is the same for all carving designs; egg and tongue, egg and dart, gadrooning, acanthus leaf, french bead (ball and sausage), or rose and ribbon. With dividers measure the width of the ovolo from angle to angle and reset to half the measurement, for example, a mould $\frac{1}{2}$in wide will have dividers set at $\frac{1}{4}$in. Mark the centre of the length of the mould to be carved and working from this centre strike off the measurement along the full length of the mould, and put a square line across the mould at these points. No further setting out is required, the carving tools mark the rest of the shape as they cut, Fig. 96.

Egg and dart mould
Select a carving gouge which fits accurately the curve of the mould but is a little less than its overall width, place one point of the cutting edge of the gouge square to the top end of the line on one side of the centre line and curving in towards it and, with the gouge held vertical, cut down to approximately one-third of the depth of the ovolo. Tilt the gouge until it is lying at right-angles to the centre of the circumference of the

ovolo and extend the cut until the nearest point of the cutting edge meets the lowest point of the centre line. Place the cutting edge of the gouge at the top end of the mould to the same curve as the first cut but approximately $\frac{1}{8}$in further away from the centre line (this size will vary a little depending on the size of the mould) and cutting at a slight angle remove a wedge-shaped piece from the top part of the mould. Repeat the operation at the line on the opposite side of the centre line, Fig. 96. This is the outline for the egg and should be repeated over the length of the mould but missing one full width of the mould between each egg. At least 1in of the mould at each end should also be left uncarved at this stage because of matching the mould to the original.

Lay the cutting edge of the same gouge up to the centre line on each egg, cut away the waste timber to form a quarter-round on one-half of the egg, reverse the chisel and repeat the operation on the other half. The front elevation of the egg should now show as a half-round and is complete, Fig. 97. The dart is now partly formed.

To complete it take the same gouge which was used to form the egg and lay the cutting edge with one point on the centre line of the dart and the other point in the angle of the bottom quirk and about $\frac{1}{8}$in short of the point of the wing and with the gouge at right-angles to the curve of the mould cut down with the top point of the gouge. Gradually bring the gouge up into a vertical position cutting to a depth of approximately two-thirds of the depth of the mould at the high point. Do not allow the point of the gouge to go below the level of the quirk at the bottom end.

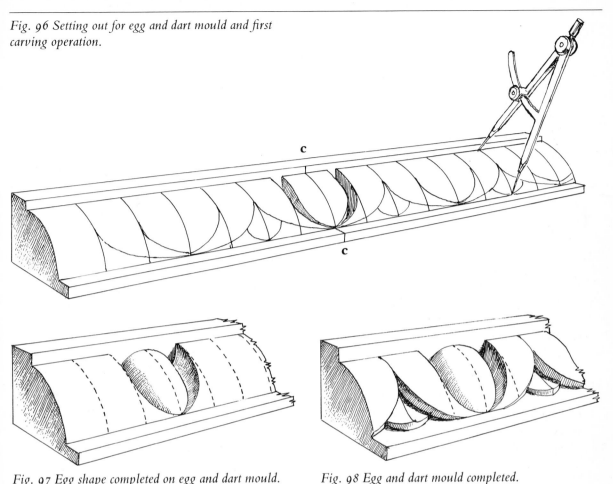

Fig. 96 Setting out for egg and dart mould and first carving operation.

Fig. 97 Egg shape completed on egg and dart mould.

Fig. 98 Egg and dart mould completed.

Using the same gouge cut away the waste wood to the two-thirds depth, and making a final cut into the third which is left, working from the top centre to the wing with the gouge held at an angle of approximately 30 degrees, so leaving a high point in the centre. Select a carving gouge which will cut approximately half a circle and with the two points of its circumference touching the wings and the centre of it to the quirk of the mould, cut down to the depth of the flat of the quirk. Using the skew chisel clean up the top area between the dart and the egg making it level to the vertical at the top end of the mould.

Trim out any feather in the other angles and the carving is now completed, Fig. 98. The minimum of glass or garnet papering should be done, often all that is necessary is a good brush over with a soft bristle brush.

There are a number of variations to the egg and dart mould but the setting out for all of them is the same and most of them are only slightly different in the detail of the wings.

Egg and tongue mould

The setting out for this carved mould is exactly the same as that for the egg and dart (working from a centre line, mark square lines across the mould at a distance of half the width of the curve of the mould apart. The eggs, however, are spaced only half a mould width apart instead of the full width which is required for the egg and dart, Fig. 99. To cut and shape the eggs follow the instructions given above for the egg and dart mould. To shape the half-width area, to form the tongue between the eggs, select a gouge which will cut a half circle with the two points of its circumference touching the outline of the eggs on

Fig. 99 Egg and tongue mould.

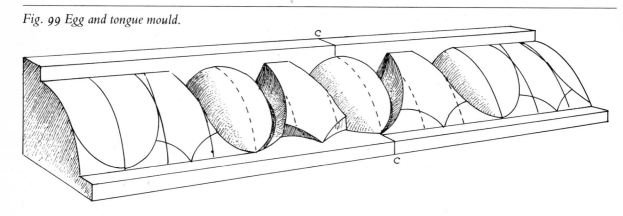

Fig. 100 Gadrooned mouldings.

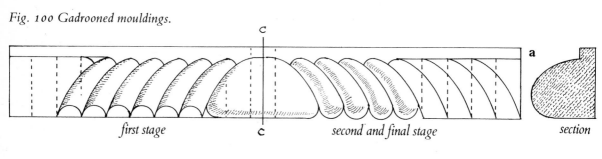

c

c

a

first stage   *second and final stage*   *section*

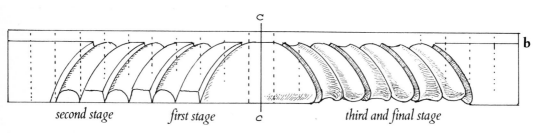

c

c

b

second stage   *first stage*   *third and final stage*

Fig. 101 Acanthus leaf worked at corner to complete egg and dart moulding.

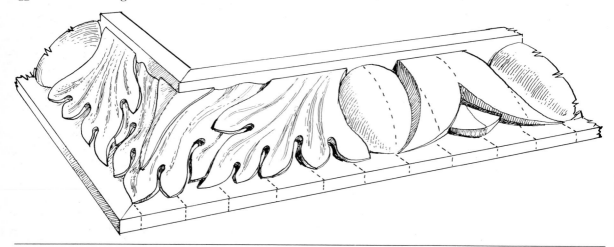

each side and the centre on the line of the quirk. Using it in a reverse position cut a quarter circle hollow on each side of the centre of the tongue and with the skew chisel clean up the areas between the eggs and the tongues. This, the most simple of the egg and tongue moulds, is now complete. There are a number of variations to the tongue but all of them are set out in the same way and none of them are difficult to execute.

Gadrooned mould

The setting out for this mould is the same as that used for the egg and dart/tongue moulds, half the width of the mould marked off over the length of the mould and squared across it. This mould can be either ovolo or a thumb mould, but is more often worked on a thumb mould.

When a thumb mould is being carved, select a chisel which fits the upper curve of the mould, and is approximately the width of the mould including the nosing, although if it is a little larger it does not matter. If, however, it is an ovolo which is being carved it must be a little less than the width of the mould. Set one point of the cutting edge on the line at the side of centres where it joins the top quirk and the other point to the line one width away (to the second line, not to the half width). With the carving chisel held vertically cut down to approximately one-quarter of the thickness of the mould and pivoting the chisel, extend the cut to the front edge of the mould. Repeat this operation at every half width over the length of the mould with the curve sloping from the top to the left on the left side of the centre and the reverse way on the right. With the same chisel, round over the face of each member, rounding the outside edge of the large centre one to match the curve of the others. A carver's back-bend chisel may be used for the concave shape of the curves, if preferred, but should not be used for the convex face because it will tear the grain of the timber, Fig. 100A.

With a carving chisel which fits the half-round at the front edge of the members, nose over the front edge of each member to form approximately a quarter sphere to complete the carving.

The gadrooned mould described here is a simple one which is easy to work, but there are a number of variations all of which are set out in the same way, by measuring off in half widths. Another which is effective and fairly easy to work is formed by using the same chisel which was used for the curves on the previous mould. Start by marking the positions and shapes of the curves only, and then use a carver's V-tool to cut along these curves to about a quarter of the depth of the mould. With the carving gouge which was used to mark the curves, round over the edges of the centre member and every alternative member over the length of the mould, and with a carver's front-bent chisel which matches the curve of these rounds work a hollow into the members between those rounded and make the front edge of them concave. With the same chisel, nose over the round members to form approximately a quarter sphere, the mould is now complete except for cleaning up in the angles with a skew chisel, Fig. 100B.

Acanthus leaf

Acanthus leaf carving is usually used at the angle corners of doors, chairs and stool frames because of the difficulty of matching up moulds which have been decorated with egg and tongue or egg and dart carving at the joints. This does not require any extra setting out, the half-width of the mould lines will suffice, also the chisels used for carving the egg and dart/tongue will be the only chisels needed apart from a veiner to put the veins in the leaves. The important thing is that the leaves are carved in shallow relief so that they appear to be laid on the ovolo mould rather than carved into it, Fig. 101. If the carver prefers he can use narrower chisels for working the outline of the leaves but the curve of the chisels should fit the circumference of the ovolo mould to produce nice flowing lines in the shapes of the leaves, any loops at the back end of the points of the leaves are done with the veining chisel. Before attempting to do any cutting, sketch out roughly the proposed outline of the leaves using the half-width mould lines to position the points and shape of the leaves, and with the gouges which fit nearest to the sketched lines make the first incisions and release a wedge of timber round the outside edges by cutting in at an angle of 45 degrees with a second cut. When this operation

Fig. 102 Acanthus leaf carving on ogee mould.

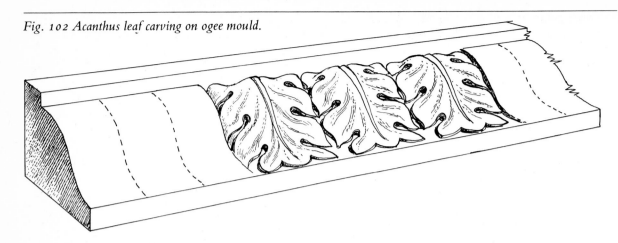

Fig. 103 Gadrooning on ogee mould.

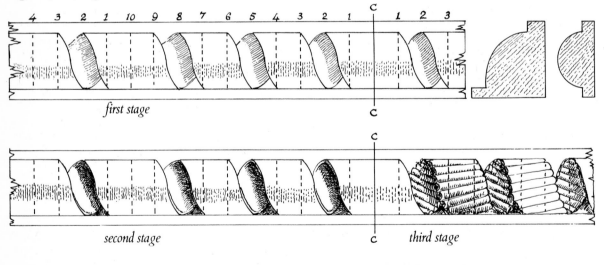

quarter width   half width   section

Fig. 104 Carving rose and ribbon mould.

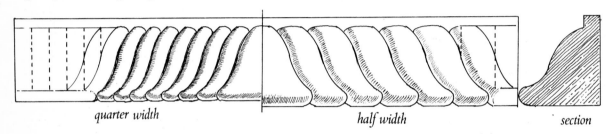

first stage

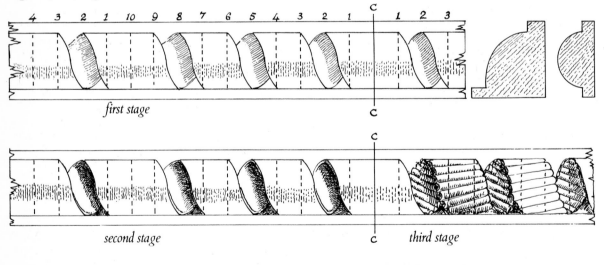

second stage   third stage

fourth and fifth stage.

has been completed over the full length required, pare away the timber round the edges to flatten them into the background and to give thickness to the carvings. Hollows can now be worked as required from the points of the leaves running towards the stalk. They should be shallow and should not touch the outside edge of the leaf shape. When these have been completed a small carver's veining chisel can be used to put in the lines of the veins which should never touch the leaf outline, or each other. If a raised vein is desired on any part, for example at the mould mitre, this is achieved by cutting on each side of the centre line with a carver's V-tool and then levelling out the outside edge of the V-cut until it curves smoothly into the flat of the leaf.

Acanthus leaf carving of ogee moulds

For a true ogee mould the shape and size of the hollow and the round should be the same, and the chisels used for carving it will give the best results if they, too, are the same circumference shape. The setting out for the ogee is the same as that for the ovolo, with half the mould width marked off on the length and squared across. Starting at the centre of the mould sketch in the shape of leaf desired using the half-width measurements to position it. With gouges which fit nearest to the shapes make the first incisions. It may not be necessary to sketch in any more than the first leaf, the others can be shaped by carefully marking in their outline with the gouges. Continue working as for the ovolo mould, Fig. 102.

Gadrooning carved on ogee moulds

This mould is worked in exactly the same way as the gadrooned ovolo mould, with the chisels fitting the hollow and the round, but the setting out can either be lines across the mould at half its width, or lines across at a quarter of the width, according to the size and shape desired, Fig. 103.

Rose and ribbon carving on ovolo or bead mould

The setting out for this mould is the same as that for other ovolo moulds. Lines half the width of the mould are squared across over the length of the mould. If worked on a bead mould the setting out is also half-width lines squared across the mould. The line in the central position of the

length of the mould will be the central position of the first rose. Select a carving gouge which fits the circumference and is approximately half the width of the mould. Holding it vertically with its convex side towards the centre of the mould, place one point of the cutting edge at the top point of the third line to the left of the centre line of the mould, and the other point of the cutting edge over the central position between line 3 and line 2. Cut down to approximately one-fifth of the depth of the mould. Lying in the same cut, pivot the chisel forward away from the top quirk to an angle of approximately 45 degrees and cut in until the top cutting point is level with the vertical face of the quirk. Reverse the chisel and with one point of the cutting edge in the first cut and the other over the position where the second line from the centre of the mould joins the lower quirk, and again with the chisel at 45 degrees cut in until the lower point of the cutting edge is touching the lowest point of line 2.

Repeat this operation from line 6 to line 5 and from line 9 to line 8. Line 10 is the centre of the next flower and counting from it will be the same as from centre of the mould. When this operation has been completed over the left half of the mould, go back to the centre and with the chisel lying horizontal, with its concave side towards the mould centre and its lowest cutting point at the lowest point of the first line to the left of centre, and its high point central between lines 1 and 2, cut in to one-fifth of the depth of the mould. Pivot the chisel upwards to approximately 45 degrees and cut in until the lowest cutting point is level with the quirk. Reverse the chisel, and with its lowest point in the first cut, and its high point over the highest point of line 2, cut in at an angle of 45 degrees until the high point of the chisel touches the high point of line 2. Repeat this operation from line 4 to line 5 and from line 7 to line 8. Allowing for line 10 to be the centre of the rose, line 1 will be the first line behind it and the operation is repeated up to line 8 and so on, until half the mould is covered. On the right side of the centre the same operations are repeated but with the chisel vertical at the high points of lines 1, 2, 4, 5, 7 and 8, and horizontal on the low points of lines 2, 3, 5, 6, 8 and 9. Line 10 will again be the centre of the rose.

Use about a half-mound width carver's No. 3 gouge to remove the waste timber between the cuts. First cut out a wedge-shaped piece to the depth of the cut working from right to left, Fig. 104, and then from left to right. Leave approximately $\frac{1}{16}$ in of timber on the top and bottom faces at the quirks for the ribbon returns. With the gouge which was used for the original cuts, round over the top ends, curving down from right to left holding the chisel horizontal and at the bottom end curving in from left to right with the chisel held vertically. With a No. 5 carving gouge, hollow out the bottom of the channels made to give the concave effect of the roll of the ribbon. With a small veining chisel flute across the ribbon to give the effects of folds or creases, and with the same chisel undercut the edges of the outward curving ribbon to take away the thick appearance.

With a carver's gouge, which will strike a circle with a diameter one-quarter of the width of the mould, cut the outline of the flower centre and remove a wedge-shaped piece round it to a depth of approximately one-fifth of the depth of the mould. With the gouge, which was used for the ogee shape of the first ribbon operation, cut the outlines of the four side petals, not the top and bottom centre petals, and remove the surplus timber round them. The top and bottom petals have a high centre point the same as the centre section of the dart on the egg and dart mould and they are worked in the same way. The four side petals have a shallow hollow worked in them and the vein effect is done with the small veining tool. A carver's skew chisel can be used to clean into the angles and down to the faces at the sides of the quirks, and the mould is then complete.

CHIP (INCISED) AND RELIEF CARVING

To take a copy of the design of chip carving or carving in shallow relief, place a piece of strong white paper over the original carving and fix it in position with fine pins. Rub over the surface with cobbler's heel-ball or with wax crayon and this will reproduce the details and outlines of the design on the paper. Remove the paper and add, free-hand, any details of the design which do not show clearly. Place the paper carefully in position on the new timber to be carved and pin it down at two diagonal corners. Slide carbon paper under the pattern and pin down the other two corners. With an HB pencil trace carefully over all the lines of the design to reproduce them on the wood with the carbon. If the design is repetitive it is not necessary to take a rubbing of the whole length, only a complete section, but the length of the section should be carefully marked on the paper and the timber marked off with this measurement over the length of the board to be carved, so that no errors are made when positioning the pattern.

Select chisels which fit all the curves of the design accurately. Cut down at right-angles to the surface and using the appropriate chisel, make the vertical cuts in the new timber to the depth required. If the carving is deeply incised into the surface it is advisable, where possible, first to cut close along the waste side of the line with a carver's V-tool. This removes pressure and stops bruising back into the timber that is to be retained. When all the vertical cuts have been made, a wedge-shaped piece can be removed by holding the appropriate chisel at an angle of approximately 80 degrees to the timber surface and cutting towards the outline cuts. The main part of the surface shaping can now be done with the gouges which have been chosen by fitting to the original surfaces to make sure of the correct shape. The background, if any, can be adjusted to depth and levelled with a carver's grounding chisel. If necessary, the background levels can be made more accurate by using a square-edge scraper cutter in a scratch-stock, but on particularly early oak furniture the background surfaces are uneven and any restoration should be the same.

To take a pattern of a carving on a cabriole knee it is necessary to take rubbings of both halves of the knee separately, unless, of course, one half is a reverse repeat of the other half when a rubbing for one half only is necessary. Place one edge of the paper accurately into the angle where the curve of the knee joins the square at the top of the leg, and fix the paper in position with two pins just inside the top edge of the paper. If the carving is a reversed repeat on the other half of the knee, place a piece of carbon paper under the pattern paper with the carbon face uppermost, facing the paper. Fix the lower edge of the pattern paper so that it fits firmly over the curve of the knee, but laying along one side of the knee only. Mark at the top edge of the paper pattern the position of the front corner of the square at the top of the leg. Now take the rubbing with a wax crayon or heel-ball, at the same time steadying the paper with the fingers of the other hand. This will give a rubbing of the complete half of the carving on one side of the paper, and the carbon paper will have given a complete reverse rubbing. After removing the paper pattern, check and mark in free-hand any details which are missing or not clear, keeping the carbon paper underneath so that the reverse repeat is marked too.

The pattern can now be positioned on the knee of the new leg, with the top edge of the paper in the angle of the knee and the leg square and the point previously marked to the front edge of the leg square. Fix the top edge of the paper with pins and place the carbon underneath it, but this time with the carbon face to the timber, and pin down the lower edge of the paper. Then go over the pattern design carefully with an HB pencil, steadying the paper with the fingers of the other hand, and repeat the operation on the other half of the knee with the carbon design uppermost. If the design is not a repeat on each half of the knee, then a second pattern should be taken. It is not advisable to bend the pattern paper round the knee to try and take both halves on the same piece. It is much more accurate to do the two separately.

When carving, first cut round but just clear of the outlines with a carver's V-tool, in depth to a little less than the original carving. With chisels which fit the original carving accurately, cut round the marked outlines. With an almost flat gouge such as a $\frac{3}{4}$in No. 3, carefully pare away the timber round the outside edges of the shaping until it stands above the knee level in the correct relief. It is only necessary to pare away from the outlines to a distance of about $\frac{1}{2}$in to $\frac{3}{4}$in and tapering out to nil. The carving can now be completed by first making all the cuts which are at right-angles to the face of the knee. Make sure that the chisels fit the shape of the original accurately, if they do not, the appearance of the carving will be completely changed.

CARVING IN THE ROUND

When copying a figure or similar, at least two patterns are required, one of a front elevation, and one of a side elevation. Sometimes a plan is also required. An accurate way to get these is to take photographs and have them enlarged to the size of the figure. The procedure for marking out the patterns on to the timber is similar to that for cabriole legs. Square up the timber to size with a face side mark on the worst face, and a face edge mark on the worst edge. If using photographs as patterns, go over the face outlines with a piece of carbon underneath, face up, to give an imprint on the back of the print. Lay the front elevation pattern face down on the face side of the timber with the extreme edge of the photographed figure to the face edge of the timber. It makes it easier to do this if the print is cut away close up to the side of the figure. Fix it at one edge with pins, slide carbon paper underneath, carbon side down, and mark round the outlines on the back of the print with a pointed dowel (a pencil thickens the lines and may cause detail to be lost). Do the same with the side elevation but with the pattern laid on the face edge and close up to the face side of the timber.

Using the band-saw, cut along the outline of the front elevation using the same technique as described for a cabriole leg, not cutting off the pieces of waste completely, Fig. 58. Then cut out the shape on the side elevation completely; the pieces left on from cutting the front elevation can then be removed. A certain amount of overall shaping can now be done using spokeshaves, rasps and files. It is then best to concentrate on one section at a time starting, if a figure, at the head and shoulders, all the time making sure that the chisels fit the parts of the original which are being copied accurately, Fig. 54. When carving in the round it is necessary to be able to hold the carving firmly but also to be able to swing it into any position which will make the carving easier. The carver's vice is similar in shape to the engineer's, but is made of wood so that if the cutting edge of a chisel touches it, no damage will be caused to the chisel. The vice is fixed to the bench with only one bolt so that it can be spun round into any position. An alternative to the carver's vice is to fix a wood-jaw handscrew down to the bench with a wood block across the jaws which is bolted down through the bench top. The carving can then be gripped in the front of the jaws and pivoted or adjusted in the same way as in the carver's vice, Fig. 105.

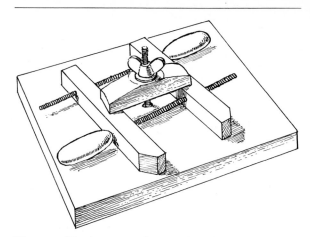

Fig. 105 Handscrew used as carving vice.

THE CARVER'S BENCH

The correct height for a carver's bench is the distance from the floor to the underside of the elbow when standing upright with the forearm bent, but the restorer may not feel it is necessary to have a special carving bench and may not have the space for one. It is, however, very tiring to work at a furniture maker's bench height if there is a lot of carving to do, and an extension which can be fitted on top of the bench is a great help.

USES OF THE PAPER-BOARD

Carving frets, small rosettes and other items which are difficult to hold in a cramp or vice may be glued on to a paper-board where they can be held firmly until the carving is completed and then easily removed by sliding the blade of a thin palette knife under them, see page 126.

Frets
The timber for frets should first be cut and dressed to net size and glued, face side up, to the paper-board. The rubbing or design should be made on thin paper and fixed with thin glue size on to the timber. Using a carver's V-tool cut round all the waste timber areas, just clear of the design lines and piercing through the timber to the paper-board. This will prevent damage to the fret design when the final cutting is done. With carving chisels which have been carefully

selected to fit the original accurately, or the design shapes if there is no original, cut along all the design lines with the chisels held in a vertical position at right-angles to the board. If the frets have carving on their faces remove the design paper with a damp cloth and carve as required. It is usual for this to be done free-hand but the design can be sketched on to the timber if it is felt necessary. The main thing is that if copying an original, the chisels which are used are checked on it for shape.

Rosettes
These are often ogee moulded on their faces, and this shaping should be done before commencing the carving. If they are round, the shape can be worked on the lathe, by gluing them on to a paper-faced board fixed to the lathe faceplate. If they are square they can be moulded in a length by planes or by machine, and then cut off to size and the cross-grain returns worked by gluing them together on a paper-board and shaping them all at the same time. If only one or two are required it will probably be easiest to work them with carving chisels, but the shape must be accurate. When setting out for carving the rosettes, all that is necessary is to divide them up into segments of four, five or six, or multiples (eight, ten or twelve). Other details can be worked directly with the chisels in much the same way as they are used when carving moulds,

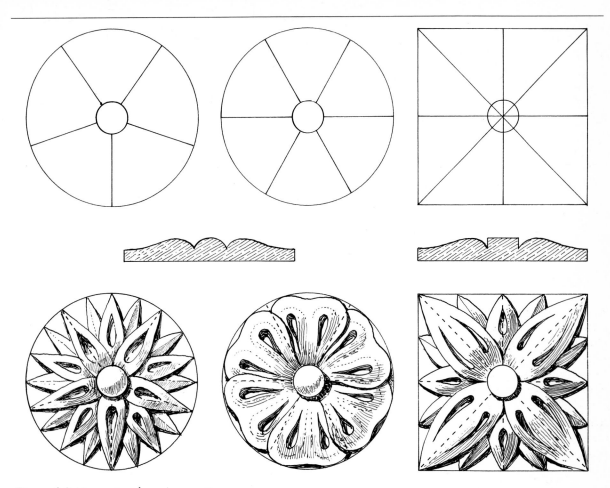

Fig. 106 Setting out and carving rosettes.

and if reproducing from an original the chisel shapes should be checked against it for accuracy, Fig. 106. When carving the veins on leaves and petals they should never be joined to each other, nor should they extend to the edge of the leaf or petal. All petal and leaf edges should be undercut so that they appear light and delicate but this should not be over done or it will make them easily damaged.

Missing pieces of carving

Restoring small pieces of carving which are missing such as parts of acanthus leaves, husks, petals, etc., is made easier using a paper-board. First the joint fitting the new piece to the old should be made, and the contour of the face of the original marked on to the joint face of the new piece; by doing this the face of the new piece can be carved leaving only minor adjustments when it is fixed. The bases of the pieces to be carved must be flat so that they will fix firmly on to the paper-board but the waste wood can be trimmed off after they have been removed and before they are fixed to the original.

Wood-turning

Broken and missing lengths of turning require special techniques and jigs for the lathe.

French or bobbin bead, whether half-round or quadrant, must, of course, be turned first in the full round. If half-round is required, two pieces of timber are prepared with their width a little over the width of the original, and their thickness a little over half the width of the original. In selecting the timber it is essential that the grain is straight otherwise breakages will occur; also they should not be turned in lengths greater than about 8in because of whipping and vibration. Glue the two face sides of the timbers together with a layer of paper between them, and when the glue is set they can be dressed to octagonal section.

If the bead is quadrant, four square pieces of timber are prepared, in size a little over half the width of the original, these are glued together in pairs with paper between and when the glue is set the faces of each pair are levelled and glued together again with paper between, making certain that the two joints which were glued first are in line with each other. When the glue is set they can be dressed to octagonal section, Fig. 107.

Before fixing them in the lathe it should be noted that if the driving point of the headstock and tailstock are driven into the turning they would separate the sections, so if possible a chuck should be used at the driving end and a cup-grip mandrel at the tailstock, Fig. 108. If these are not available, then a piece of plywood should be glued and pinned on each end to receive the points, making certain that the holes in the ply to receive the points are accurately centred on the section joints of the turning.

After carefully turning the octagonal shape into a round, a special back-steady is required to support the full length of the turning, otherwise it will just shatter to pieces when it is turned into beading Fig. 109. With dividers mark off the lengths of the beads on to the timber, and with a small skew turning chisel laid edge way up with the long point side down on the T-rest, inset at the divider marks to approximately half the depth finally required. If the beading is fairly large it may be necessary to cut out a 45 degree wedge on each side of the first cut, Fig. 110a.

The final shaping of the beads is done by laying the bevel of the skew chisel flat on to the turning, with its short point at the centre of each bead and the cutting edge lying at 45 degrees away from it. Tilt the chisel until it starts to cut, and work it over to make a quarter-round, at the same time pivoting the handle of the chisel round until the blade lies at right-angles to the cut and the cutting edge is vertical to the cut. When all the beads have been quarter-rounded at one side reverse the chisel and repeat the operation on the other side, Fig. 110b. The paper joints can be separated with a thin-bladed knife.

Split turnings, such as those used for decoration of Jacobean furniture and the split columns seen on the heads of grandfather clocks, can be prepared and turned in the same way as the beading but the back-steady will probably not be necessary for them.

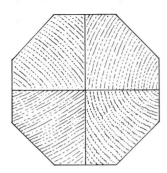

Fig. 107 Section through timber prepared with paper-lined joints for turning quadrant beading.

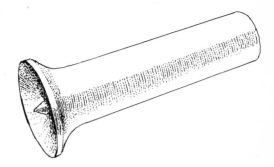

Fig. 108 Cup-style tailstock turning grip.

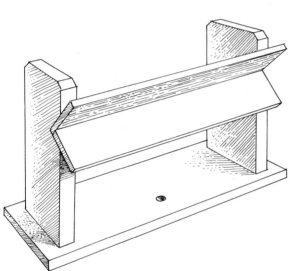

Fig. 109 Back steady for fine turnings.

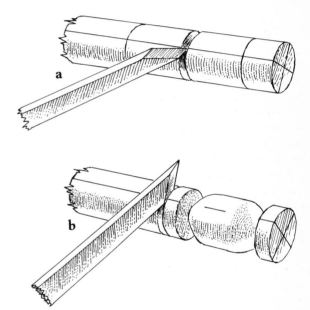

Fig. 110 Bead turning.

Finials should first be turned between centres to remove most of the waste timber and to shape the dowel pin. The dowel pin should then be fixed into a driving chuck and the back-steady, Fig. 109, fitted so that it supports the point and the neck so that the final shaping can be done without any danger of vibration or breakage. When part of a turning is broken or missing, the replacement can usually be turned between centres with a jointing pin on them. Whenever possible butt joints (end grain to end grain) should be made close to a bead or quirk on the original turning, so that the repair shows as little as possible, Fig. 111. When marking the centre

for boring to receive the pin in the original, the special centring jig should be used. When turning a new foot on a broken leg, the turning should always be left longer than the net size and cut to exact length when the leg has been fixed to the chair, stool, or cabinet. This length is marked by balancing a straight-edge on the bottoms of the two original legs at one end of the piece of furniture, and laying a straight-edge on the bottom of the original leg at the other end and up to the side of the new leg and adjusting until the straight-edges show parallel to each other. The leg can then be marked and cut to length, Fig. 112.

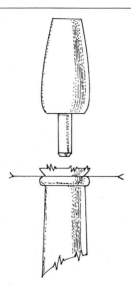

Fig. 111 Fixing new leg section.

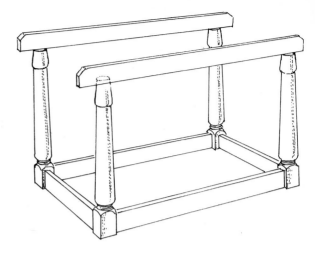

Fig. 112 Squaring new leg section to correct length.

When there is no bead or quirk which can be used to blind the butt joint on a turning, then a splice should be used instead, and it is necessary to make a card pattern of the shape so that the new section can be checked for true alignment as the splice is being made. The splice should be made with the new piece of timber still in the square shape, it should then be glued and left to set. The centres for turning should then be marked by laying the turning on the pattern with the face side of the new piece down; with a square, mark up the centre line of the pattern across the end of the new piece and also the end of the old, then turn the turning with the face edge of the new down and mark the ends again using the square, Fig. 34. There is usually some shrinkage in old turnings so that they are not truly

round. The new section should be turned down to the widest part of the old and the final shape finished with a fine-set spokeshave.

When setting calipers for copying, they should fit loosely over the old turning and should fit firmly over the new, this allows for final glass-papering. It is advisable, if possible, to run the lathe the reverse way when doing the first papering because the grain has been forced over a little when the shaping was done and glass-papering in reverse will remove this. Damp down the turning with water before finally finishing, which will stop the grain lifting when it is stained and polished. The moisture should be allowed to dry out before the final papering is done with the lathe running in the right direction.

Restoring veneering

If a veneer is blistered but laying reasonably flat on its background, take a sharp needle and pierce its surface at approximately $\frac{1}{4}$in intervals, then spread animal glue-size, which should be thinned down with water until it is about half the consistency of normal glue used for jointing, liberally over the whole surface of the blister. Take a hot flat iron, e.g. an electric clothes iron is suitable, and lay it carefully on to the size but prevent it touching the veneer if possible; the heat will force the size through the needle holes, and after a few seconds the iron can be pressed down on to the veneer. It should only be held there for a short period, certainly not long enough for it to dry out the size. If the use of the iron has not relaid the blister, spread a little more size over it and lay it by working a veneer hammer over it, Fig. 113. If part of the blister still has a tendency to lift, and this can be checked by tapping over the surface with your finger, then take a small piece of cardboard or thin ply and fix it over the area with a needle point (if ply is used a piece of paper should be laid under it to stop it sticking to the veneer). When the blister is finally laid, two or three sheets of newspaper should be laid over it until it is dry to exclude the air which might lift the blister again.

If the surface being restored has a polished finish the size can be left on the surface until it is hard and dry. It will normally release itself and can then be easily brushed off, but if the surface is unpolished the size should be wiped off with a warm damp cloth. All veneers which have been relaid should be covered with layers of paper or cloth to exclude the air until they are dry.

If a blister is standing up well clear of the background, this usually means that the background timber has shrunk, and to relay the blister it is necessary to use a sharp veneer knife and a straight-edge to cut through the centre of it, following the line of the grain. Then using a small palette knife, or similar blade, put a layer of thin glue under one half of the blister and lay it with a small veneer hammer. Put a layer of glue under the other half of the blister and lay that with the veneer hammer; it will now be seen that the veneer overlaps the half laid first. Take a sharp knife and carefully cut along the edge of the overlapping half of the blister. Lift that half of the blister and remove the piece of surplus veneer underneath, then lay the half again, using a hot iron to warm the glue. Use card or ply to hold down if required and cover to exclude air.

Excessive blistering on a carcase panel is often caused by the background timber being affected by worm. Although the panel on the reverse side may only appear to be moderately affected, the face under the veneer will often be heavily honeycombed because the glue moisture attracts the worm. The veneer must be removed before the background is strengthened and levelled, but before attempting to remove the veneer, a sheet of strong paper should be fixed on to the surface with thin glue size. Then using a hot electric iron and a cloth soaked in hot water, soften the glue under the veneer approximately 2in in from the least conspicuous edge, for example the back edge. If there is polish on the veneer this should be removed from the 2in area first. As the glue is softened, a thin-bladed knife should be inserted to release the veneer. Carefully ease it up until thin,

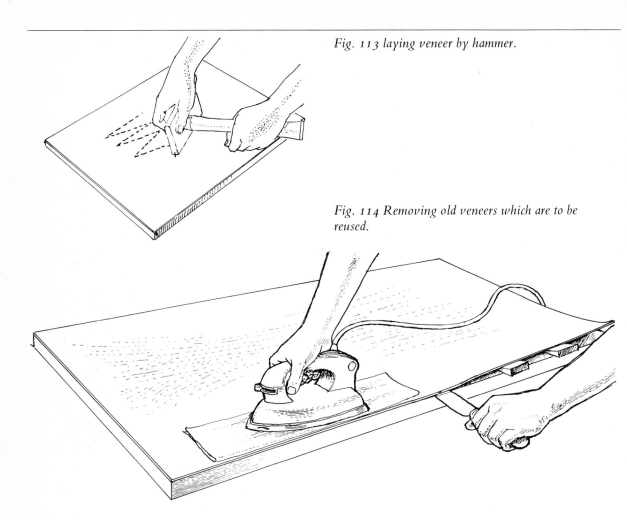

Fig. 113 laying veneer by hammer.

Fig. 114 Removing old veneers which are to be reused.

paper-covered wedges can be placed under it to stop the glue refixing it down again, Fig. 114. Now lay the panel at an angle of approximately 45 degrees with the released edge uppermost and carefully spray methylated spirits into the opening between the veneer and the panel. This will gradually spread into the glue line of the still-fixed veneer and destroy the adhesion so that it, too, can be raised with the knife and at the same time moving the wedges further in. Using this method the veneer can be removed while still retaining most of the original patina and polished finish which is most important.

Immediately after removal, the papered side of the veneer should be glued to a flat board, covered with paper and a second board and left until the glue has set. The back surface of the veneer can then be dressed over with a toothing

plane, Fig. 115, to remove old glue, etc. Replace the paper and board cover until you are ready to refix the veneer. The exposed worm-damaged surface of the panel should now be treated with glue size (see page 71). Make up a solution of thin glue size and plaster of Paris mixed to a creamy consistency, and brush it over the surface of the worm-eaten area until a sufficient number of coats have been applied to be sure that when the plaster has dried out and shrunk, it is still higher on the damaged surfaces, than the original face of the panel. There is no need to wait between the applications, they can be brushed immediately on top of each other. Cover the panel surface with paper to exclude air, and leave to set for 24 hours. When the plaster solution is hard, dress it down with a toothing plane, Fig. 115, until it is level with the original surface. Carefully remove all loose dust and finally wipe

Fig. 115 Toothing plane.

it over with a damp cloth. The veneer can now be relaid either by press or hammer.

Sometimes a panel under a veneer is so badly damaged and weakened by worm that it must be replaced. This should only happen in the most extreme cases because any replacement of original parts will devalue the furniture to some extent. Fix strong paper with glue size over the whole of the surface of the veneer including crossbands, lines, marquetry, etc., and then glue this papered side on to a flat board of ply or similar. When the glue has set, make a series of saw cuts, approximately one inch apart, across the grain of the worm-eaten timber to a depth of approximately $\frac{1}{8}$in clear of the back side of the veneer. With a chisel and mallet remove the saw-curfed timber to the depth of the saw cut. A smoothing plane can now be used to remove the rest of the surplus timber, dressing down until the glue used for the original

veneering just shows through. Now, using a toothing plane, remove the rest of the surplus timber and also the old glue. The now clean veneer should be covered with a board or paper to exclude the air until it is wanted for relaying.

Preparation of the new background timber must be done with great care, particularly if it is only veneered on the face side. The timber should match the original as closely as possible; the width should be built up with boards not more than 6in wide, the heart side of the boards must be made the face side (the side on which the veneer is going to be glued) because as the veneer dries out it shrinks and tends to pull the boards hollow on the face; but the boards will also shrink and they shrink less on the heart side than on the reverse, therefore there is a counter-pull which helps to keep the panel flat, Fig. 116.

The boards should be rub-jointed together

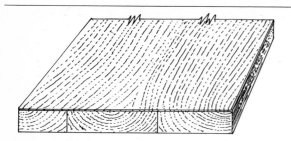

Fig. 116 Boards veneered on heart-side of panel.

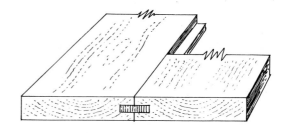

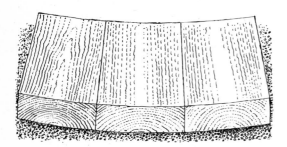

Fig. 118 Boards expanded on bed of wet sawdust.

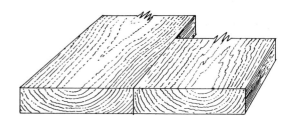

Fig. 117 A tongue and groove joint (top) and rubbed joint.

using animal glue when making up the panel, not tongued and grooved because these joints may show through the veneer, Fig. 117. When the glue has set, the panel should be dressed and the face side levelled with a toothing plane. The toothing plane is not used to make a key for the glue, as is imagined by some people; the plane iron is set very fine and as it moves over the surface it removes all high spots and makes the panel completely flat. If high spots were left, a thick layer of glue would form round them which would crystallise and cause blisters under the veneer.

The boards should now be squared up to a little over the net size and laid face down on a bed of wet sawdust which will cause the face side to expand in width making the panel convex. Leave overnight to allow the face to expand to its maximum before coating with glue size and finally cover with layers of paper to exclude the air until it is set, Fig. 118. If the panel is counter-veneered, that is veneered on both sides, the wet sawdust treatment is not required, but the grain of the counter-veneer must run in the same direction as the veneer on the face. If, however,

the veneer on the face side is a burr, with knots and the grain running in all directions, it is usual to have the grain of the counter-veneer running the opposite way to that of the panel. If the panel which is being renewed is a large one and is counter-veneered it is not usually possible to save the original counter-veneer, but with a small panel it may be possible to split the panel through with a circular saw or hand saw, and then by saw curfing the two halves both veneers can be saved.

If laying is done by veneer press all is now ready, except that the panel should be run over again with the toothing plane to remove any paper or bits which may have stuck to it. The veneer should be damped, not wetted, on the back face and placed between two boards to prevent it curling up. This moistening is necessary because the veneer will be brittle and might crack as it is being laid. Laying by press is comparatively straightforward. Glue the panel and lay the veneer carefully in position on the panel. A layer or more of paper should always be put between the press plate and the veneer in case any glue penetration should fix the panel to the plate. Glue penetration

74

can be reduced considerably if, when making up the animal glue, a heaped tablespoon of ordinary baking flour is added to every pint of the liquid. This does not weaken the glue because the flour itself is an adhesive.

Veneering by hand, using a veneer hammer, is more complicated than laying by press and requires practice. The preparation before laying is the same as for laying by press. Before starting to lay the veneer, have the following items conveniently placed so that they can quickly be picked up as needed.

> a pot of thin hot animal glue size
> a veneer hammer of convenient width
> an electric iron at medium heat
> a cotton cloth damped with water
> a pot, with hot water jacket, of hot animal glue.

The panel should be firmly fixed, with wood bench stops, to a bench where it is possible to move round it freely. Using a fairly large glue brush, spread the glue quickly on to the panel surface and lay the veneer carefully in position on top of it, pressing it firmly down with the hands. Now spread a layer of glue size over the surface of the veneer to act as a lubricant for the veneer hammer to slide easily. All the surplus glue must be removed from beneath the veneer by working from the centre to the outside edges with the veneer hammer, at the same time keeping the glue warm by periodically running over the surface with the hot iron. With one hand placed firmly over the blade of the veneer hammer, with the handle pointing towards the craftsman, and the other hand gripping the extreme end of the handle work it from side to side while at the same time drawing the hammer towards the outside edge of the veneer, Fig. 113. If the panel is a large one, start at one end gluing approximately four square feet at a time and laying it with the veneer hammer. Lift the veneer off the next section to be glued by carefully placing a wood lath under it and lifting it high enough to spread the glue, overlapping a little on to the glue of the previous area laid, and lay that with the hammer. Always remember that there must be a spread of glue size for the hammer

to work easily and that the glue must be kept warm with the iron.

When the veneer has been completely laid, put it face down on a paper-covered board to exclude the air until the glue has set, making sure first that all the surplus size has been removed with a damp cloth. If any surplus glue is left under the veneer it will crackle and form a blister. Check for blisters after you have finished laying the complete panel by tapping the surface with your fingers, pencil or a piece of dowel, and if one is found, warm it with the iron and lay it again with the hammer. If this proves unsuccessful warm a piece of ply, or similar, and fix that down on the blister with fine needle points. A layer of paper should be put under the ply to avoid it sticking to the veneer.

For restoration work it is advisable to have three or four veneer hammers, varying in size from 2 to 6in and including at least one with a carboned-wood edge (instead of metal) which is particularly useful on shaped work and also when working on an old polished surface. All hammer blades should be cleaned immediately after use as any glue allowed to set on the blade will scratch or tear the veneer.

Laying new veneer uses a similar process to relaying old, but it should be noted that for restoration work the veneer should be at least double the thickness of the modern knife-cut veneers. The veneer must first be dampened with water and placed between two flat boards until it is dry. The flat veneer can now easily be jointed up to width, either by straightening the edges using a straight-edge and a veneer knife, or fixing two veneers between two straight-edges and shooting the two at once with a try plane. The veneers should then be jointed together with brown paper tape which shrinks as it dries and pulls the joint together. After jointing, the veneers should be placed between two boards until required for laying.

REPAIRING AND PATCHING VENEERS

In selecting materials for repair work it cannot be

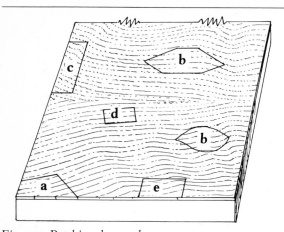

Fig. 119 Patching damaged veneers.

a *and* **b** *are correct,* **c**, **d** *and* **e** *are incorrect*

overstressed that they must be of the same species as the timbers used for the original work. For example, only Cuban and Honduras mahogany was used until approximately the end of the 18th century. So African mahogany cannot be used instead of the South American mahogany for repair work. Similarly American oak or walnut cannot be used instead of European.

It may be necessary to cut the veneers required from solid timbers in order to get the correct thickness, either by using a circular saw with a cross-cut blade (teeth about six to the inch) or a handsaw (teeth about ten to the inch). After cutting the veneer the new sawn face should be dressed and levelled with a toothing plane. This can be done by gluing the veneer on to a flat paper-faced board. When the veneer is released from the paper board it should be immediately coated on both sides with thin glue size and covered to exclude the air.

To patch up where a piece of veneer is missing, first select an area on the new veneer which is the closest match to the grain and figure of the original, and cut it so that it easily covers the damaged area. Make sure that end grain is not fitted to end grain or the joint will always show and it will also be difficult to colour, Fig. 119. Now hold the veneer up level with the eyes and look along the grain from both ends. It will show

darker from one end which means that you are looking into the grain and if planed in that direction the grain would tear-up; mark an arrow in the opposite direction to show the right way of the grain. Now do the same to the piece of furniture, in the area where the patching is going to be done, putting an arrow on the background which will be covered by the new veneer. This procedure is most important because if the veneer is reverse grained to the original it is impossible to colour match. Lay the new veneer carefully over the area to be repaired making sure that both arrows are pointing in the same direction and fix it temporarily with two or more needle points. With a veneer knife, cut carefully round the outside edges of the new veneer making sure that the knife penetrates right through the original veneer as well. Now remove the patch of new veneer and cut away the waste around the damaged area, at the same time removing any glue and dirt from the background. The new piece can now be glued in position, using a small veneer hammer to lay it, and surplus glue removed. Size should be used on the face of the veneer to lubricate for the hammer, and the patch should then be covered immediately to exclude the air.

Veneer repairs are best dressed and levelled down with a square-edged cabinet scraper with the edges not turned over with a steel as they would be for normal cabinet work. The scraper can be held in an almost vertical position and will then cut and level off the surplus material to the level of the original without cutting into it. There is also less danger of tearing the veneer with the square-edged scraper. All newly-dressed areas should be covered to exclude the air until they are coloured and polished.

Cross-banding
This is laid and fitted using the same process as for patching, making certain that the grain of all the pieces is running in the same direction. The edges of the veneer can overlap the outside edges of the panel on which they are laid, but not more than approximately $\frac{1}{8}$in, otherwise the overlap will dry and shrink too quickly causing the veneer to release from the edge of the panel. After fixing and levelling the cross-banding, it is

advisable to glue a layer of strong paper over it to reduce the possibility of shrinking at the joints.

If the panel has a decorative or line inlay between the main veneer and the cross-band, ignore it and fit the cross-band as if it did not exist. It should be left until the cross-band has been dressed and levelled, and then by routing out for it with a scratch-stock a perfect fit can be made. This would not be very easy if it were fitted before the cross-band was laid.

Decorative line inlays

These vary to such an extent that it is almost impossible to match them with ready-made stock from a dealer, so the restorer must be capable of making them. Do not attempt to make them in material of veneer thickness. It is much easier to make them in thick timber from which layers of veneer thickness can later be cut. When making up herring-bone inlay (popular in the walnut period), select a straight-grained board approximately 6in wide by 1in thick, and cut a piece off one end of it at an angle of 45 degrees, Fig. 120a. Plane the new cut edges on both pieces until they make a perfect joint with each other. Reverse the short pieces and glue it back on to the main board, mitre joining the two together. The herring-bone shape of the grain at this angle may now be cut off at the width required, Fig. 120b, and the two sawn edges planed until the piece is true and exact to size. The inlay may have straight-grained borders of the same material, or alternatively of boxwood, fruitwood or sycamore, so laths of the particular material are glued on each edge, Fig. 120c. The complete inlay can now have layers of veneer thickness cut from it using a thin, fine saw to get the maximum number of layers. The example taken is a fairly easy one, but all inlays are made on the same principle using thick material, Fig. 120d, e, f.

Oystershell inlays

These are thick veneers cut off the smaller branches of trees with pronounced annual rings such as walnut, laburnum, etc. The veneers are cut off the ends of the branches at an angle of approximately 45 degrees and cut and fitted together on the panel surface to form a shell

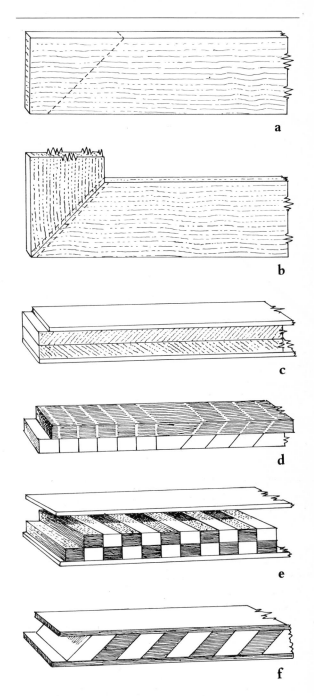

Fig. 120 Decorative line inlays.

a *and* **b** *board cut and rejointed to attain herring-bone inlay;* **c** *herring-bone inlay complete with borders;* **d** *ebony and boxwood jointed for check inlay;* **e** *making up check by reversing alternate sections;* **f** *diagonal check.*

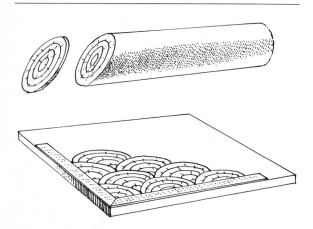

Fig. 121 Oystershell veneering.

effect, Fig. 121, intersected in a semi-geometrical design.

DYEING AND SHADING VENEERS

Veneers were dyed to various colours such as red, green, blue and black by immersing them in hot (not boiling) water to which a water soluble dye had been added. The timber usually used for this purpose was sycamore, but pear was sometimes used, particularly for black lines, and it has been noted by the author that often when pear has been used the lines have disintegrated and powdered away.

Over a period of time all these colours will have faded except, perhaps, in carcase interiors where they have been excluded from the light: the red to a pale orange, green to dirty light brown, blue to grey.

To obtain these faded shades of colour, the veneers should first be dyed with original rich colours, then placed between layers of paper to soak up the surplus moisture, and put under pressure to keep them flat until they are dry. The veneers can then be fitted and fixed into the panel and toned down in colour to match the original by coating them with a strong solution of hydrogen peroxide, or with an oxalic acid solution. Care should be taken when applying bleaches not to overlap on to any of the original.

If the bleaches alone do not have the desired effect, treat with alternate coats of ammonia and hydrogen peroxide.

After using bleach or ammonia the surfaces treated should always be rubbed over with a cloth wetted with water to neutralize the solution, but this must be dried off immediately.

Shading veneers
This is achieved by scorching them with hot sand. Fill a shallow metal tray with silver sand and heat it over a flame until it stops steaming and is really hot. The area of the veneer which requires shading is then put edgeway up into the sand. The variations of shading are produced by adjusting the veneer higher or lower into the sand.

MARQUETRY AND BUHL RESTORATION

Marquetry
Marquetry repairs are usually done by cutting and fitting each piece independently but can be done, as marquetry was done originally, by gluing together the different veneers with a layer of paper between each layer, and then cutting out the various shapes and fitting the different woods into each other to make up the complete missing area, a bit like doing a jigsaw puzzle. This method wastes a lot of veneer. The alternative is to cut each piece independently by first taking a rubbing of the area. Place a piece of strong white paper over the part which needs replacing and hold it down firmly with needle points if it is a large area. Then rub over the surface with an HB pencil working in all directions. Still holding firmly, rub over the surface again with your fore-finger. The outlines should now show up clearly in a darker shade including, usually, all the details of the pattern, because where the different pieces are jointed together the old glue stands up a little from the background. This pattern can now be used to mark out the designs on the different veneers required. Lay the paper on the veneer with a carbon paper beneath it and go over the outlines with, preferably, a fine-pointed dowel instead of

a pencil which tends to thicken the lines. The veneers are now ready for cutting. As the shapes are cut out, and a fine jeweller's piercing saw blade is better for this purpose than fret-saw blades, they should be fitted together with the back side uppermost and glued down on to a sheet of paper. Keep them covered with a flat board until the design is complete and is ready to be laid. Providing the dowel point is kept accurately on the centre of the dark outline when marking off the separate pieces, and when cutting the line is cut out completely, the pieces should fit together and fit into the damaged area without any further adjustment.

The veneers used when restoring marquetry, should be thicker than would probably be used for other work, not less than $\frac{1}{16}$in. While waiting for the new marquetry to set on the paper, the area on which it is going to be laid should be thoroughly cleaned of old glue and dirt. The easiest way to do this is with small square-edged scrapers of various widths. These are also useful for levelling the veneers when they have been laid. A $\frac{1}{16}$in square section blade scraper with a square end and fitted into a handle, Fig. 18, is needed to clean out the angle where the edges of the old veneer meet the background. The small square-edged scrapers may be used in a scratch-stock if preferred.

Blisters in wood marquetry can be relaid either by lifting the loose pieces out and cleaning them and the background before relaying or, if this is not convenient, by pin-pricking the blistered areas, covering them with glue size and using the hot iron in the same way as for ordinary veneer blisters, page 71.

Buhl restoration

Techniques for cutting and fitting are the same as those for wood marquetry, the brass, pewter, tortoiseshell, etc., being cut and shaped with a jeweller's piercing-saw. This also applies when cutting ivory, mother-of-pearl or any other non-wood material. Because of opposing expansion and contraction of wood and metals it is necessary to use a special glue for fixing. Andre Charles Boule (1642-1732) from whom the name buhl is derived, mixed his glue with

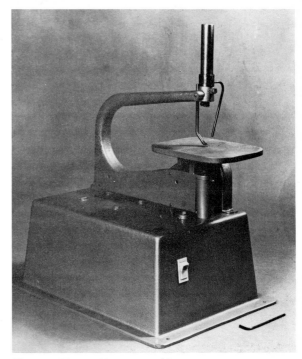

Fig. 122 Fret or jig-saw machine.

the water in which garlic had been boiled, but in England urine was used instead of water. This had the effect not only of slightly corroding the metal which made it key, but also the glue, instead of setting brittle, set only to a leathery consistency which allowed for the movement of the wood against the metal without breaking the adhesion. A modern glue which the author has found to have this leather quality is *Tretbond 404*, but it must be thinned down with the special thinners from its almost treacle consistency to that of thin cream, otherwise the metal just lies on the top of it and the glue sets under it like a layer of rubber. If, when restoring tortoiseshell, there is colour beneath it, matching pigment colour should be added to the glue.

When cutting materials for buhl work it is preferable to use a machine fret or jig saw. The upper moving section to which the saw blade is fixed should have a piston action, not a rocker-arm as this allows too much side-whip, Fig. 122.

The bore in the usual fret saw table is about $\frac{1}{2}$in in diameter and if very delicate fine designs are being cut, the saw teeth tend to drag them

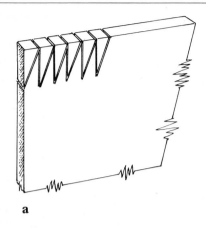

a

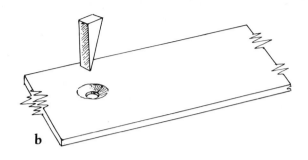

b

Fig. 123 Cutting pins for buhl work.

through the bore and bend or break them. It is advisable to fit a wood bed over the original with a bore the width of the saw through it. When cutting stringing for narrow line inlays, fit a width guide to the saw table, otherwise it is almost impossible to saw accurately in a straight line with these very fine saws. Before cutting the brass, and again before laying, it should be annealled by holding it over a flame, otherwise it is likely to be rather springy and difficult to cut and fix down. A convenient thickness for the materials used for buhl or similar work should be not less than 20 gauge. Metal thinner than this causes problems with cutting and shaping. Before laying brass or tortoiseshell it should be keyed on the back by scarring it with an old file or needle point.

If it is necessary to permanently pin down the metal, and this should only be done in extreme circumstances such as when a large sheet or strips 1in or more in width is laid, brass nails or pins should never be used. Brass wedges with a square head and approximately $\frac{3}{8}$in in length should be cut from the same metal as that which is being laid, Fig. 123a. The brass to be laid should be bored to receive the pins not less than $\frac{1}{4}$in from the edges, with a drill diameter the same size as the brass sheet thickness (20 gauge $= \frac{1}{32}$in). After boring, the holes should be countersunk to a depth which will give a measurement at the top edge of the countersink of approximately the size of the diagonals of the wedges (with wedges cut from 20 gauge the measurement would be $\frac{3}{64}$in), Fig. 123b. Using a

small rivetting hammer, drive the wedges into the holes and as they are driven a head will form on them which will fill the countersunk area. When the heads are levelled off with files and square-edged scrapers they should be barely noticeable.

When dressing and levelling buhl-type marquetry diemakers rifflers can be used for the initial dressing, and the final dressing and levelling should be done with square-edged scrapers which, if slightly curved on the length of the edge, will help to avoid lifting the inlays. This should be followed by burnishing with 000 or 0000 gauge wire wool soaked with linseed oil. For the final burnishing a paste of fine crocus powder and raw linseed oil should be used for the tortoise-shell and the mahogany; and for ebony and other dark surfaces use charcoal powder instead of the crocus. Never use glass, garnet, or emery paper, because the metal dust from papering will coat-over the tortoiseshell, ebony, or mahogany and it is difficult to remove. After burnishing the marquetry surfaces should be polished with wax, not with shellac, which will chill on the metal surfaces and cause a creamy bloom.

If the original metal is loose and is lifting and has probably been kinked and twisted by use and when dusting, it should be folded back, over a piece of dowel or a pencil to avoid further kinking, at a convenient position. The background can then be cleaned of old glue and dirt and the metal laid back again as close as possible to its original position. Where it has

Fig. 124 Veneer presses.

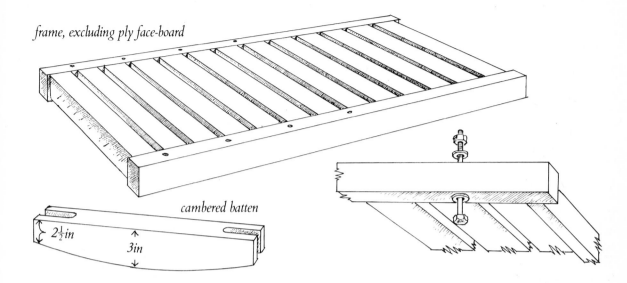

frame, excluding ply face-board

cambered batten

$2\frac{1}{2}$in

3in

been stretched through repeated bending and straightening over a period, it should be bowed up until it shortens into its correct position. Now carefully slide a piece of $\frac{1}{8}$in lead sheet under it, and with a small leather-faced mallet, Fig. 14, tap on each side of the bowed-up areas until the metal is slightly impressed into the lead. With a finger on the impressed area on each side of the bowed section, tap with the mallet on top of the bow until it is level. This should shorten it off, but it may require more than one treatment in this way. When satisfied that the metal is flat and correctly positioned, carefully fold it over again, using the dowel, and apply the special glue on the background. Lay the metal back in position, and when certain that it is entered into the space made for it. It can be tapped down firmly into its background with the leather-faced mallet. Neither a hammer nor wooden mallet should be used for this purpose because they would expand the metal.

VENEER PRESSES

There are two methods of making inexpensive veneer presses which are easy and convenient to manipulate, providing there is space to store them. The first is made from a pine frame using $4\frac{1}{2}$in ×

3in standard joinery timber, morticed and tenoned together, with the mortice holes in the $4\frac{1}{2}$in face, and with an even number of 6in × 2in muntins, not more than 1in apart, morticed and tenoned so that their face side is flush with the face side of the frame, Fig. 124.

The width of the frame should not be less than 24in, and the most useful length is 6ft, but this can be reduced if space is not available. The face side of the frame should be dressed with a try plane until it is level and clear of twist. Then a sheet of 1in ply or blockboard, fitting the size of the frame, should be glued firmly down on the face. Finally a fine-set toothing plane should be used on the face of the blockboard to remove any bumps and unevenness.

Holes should now be bored in the centre of the stiles, the first holes in a central position between the rails and the muntins, and then at every space between the muntins along the length of the frame on each stile. The holes are to receive $\frac{1}{2}$in bolts which should be long enough to protrude at least 4in out of the top side of the blockboard, and should have about 3in of thread for the nuts. Two washers approximately 2in in diameter should be supplied for each bolt, one under the head and the other under the nut.

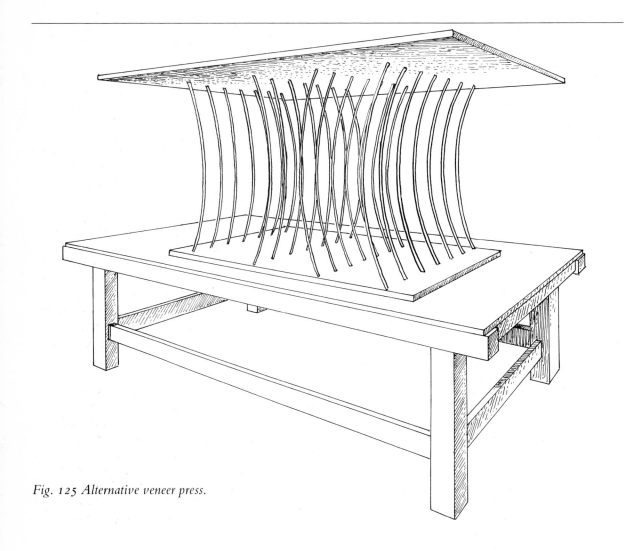

Fig. 125 Alternative veneer press.

Battens should be made from 4in × 2in pliable hardwood (ash, birch, beech) which are slotted at each end to fit under the bolt washers to apply the pressure on the back side of the panel which is being veneered. The slots at one end of the battens should be long enough for it to slide under the washer until it is clear of the edge of the washer on the opposite bolt. This avoids having to remove the nuts completely when fitting the battens in position. The bottom face of the batten should have a camber of approximately $\frac{1}{2}$in along its length, so that pressure is exerted first on the centre and, as it is tightened down, pressure is gradually distributed right to the outside edge and in so doing removes the surplus glue from under the veneer, Fig. 124.

The second method can only be used if the workshop has a strong low ceiling. A frame the same as the one described above is made, excluding only the bolt holes. On the ceiling over the bench on which the frame is laid, when in use, will be fixed a 1in ply board the same size as the frame. Two or three dozen $\frac{3}{4}$in malacca canes are required, 2in–3in longer in length than the distance from the top of the frame to the ceiling panel. When the panel has been laid veneer side down on the caul-covered frame the canes are sprung in between the ceiling panel and the veneer panel, starting at the centre and placing the canes not more than twelve inches apart. They will exert sufficient pressure to squeeze out the surplus glue to the outside edges.

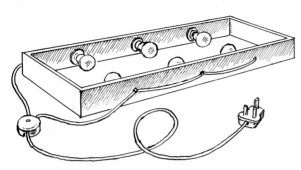

Fig. 126 Caul heater.

Straight-grained hardwood dowel may be used instead of the canes, Fig. 125. A caul which can be heated and laid on the face of the ply-covered frame of the press is necessary. This keeps the glue warm on the veneer panel which is being laid, and the best material for this purpose is $\frac{1}{8}$in thick zinc plate because it retains the heat well. The plate need not be in one piece, but if in two or more pieces, for convenience of handling, care must be taken that they fit well together at the joints.

The zinc cauls can be heated easily by making a frame in box form, the same size as the caul, and fitting a number of electric light bulbs inside it. The cauls should not be heated by any means whereby a naked flame might touch them, because zinc has a very low melting point, Fig. 126.

Sand-bag cauls may be used for laying veneers on shaped surfaces. These are made by filling a strong linen bag three-quarters full with silver sand. The bag should then be heated in an oven to remove the moisture from the sand. The oven can be fairly hot but care should be taken that it is not over-heated so that it scorches and damages the linen bag. When the bag is thoroughly dry and steam has stopped rising from it, take the shaped panel and press it firmly on to the bag working it into the sand until the two fit closely together and then put the bag back in the oven to keep it hot. The panel can now be glued and the veneer fitted in position on to it. Remove the bag carefully from the oven and place it on the bed of the press. Lay the veneered panel in position on top of it and apply the pressure.

If no oven is available the sand bag can be heated on a hot-plate. It retains its heat for a considerable time so it is not necessary to rush the laying of the veneer. Care should be taken to make sure that the bag is completely sealed after the sand is put into it. Any escaping sand may cause damage to the veneer. When the bag is not in use it should be kept in a damp-proof container such as a plastic bag, to avoid it collecting damp again.

Restoring surface decoration

PREPARING AND RESTORING COMPO DECORATION

Compo, as the name implies, is a mixture composed of plaster of Paris and animal glue. It was used for decoration in England in the 18th and 19th centuries as an alternative to carving, particularly when there was a lot of repetition in the decoration because it could reduce the cost of manufacture. It should not be confused with gesso, a mixture of glue and whitening, which was applied on the surface of wood carvings, etc., to give a clean smooth surface for gilding, lacquering and painted decoration.

The carver first made originals of the decoration required. These were either made in wood, or roughly moulded by hand in compo and the final details worked and shaped with carving tools after the compo had set. The wood patterns were coated with varnish and rubbed down until they were perfectly smooth. The compo surfaces were coated with a solution of resin mixed with hot water which hardened the surface and reduced the danger of breakage and also smoothed down any unevenness.

The compo was prepared in a particular way to get a smooth even mixture. First a glue size was prepared which, when cold, would be the same consistency as table jelly. With the size at body heat, the plaster of Paris was gradually added, a little at a time, stirring the size continually to avoid the mixture going lumpy, until it had a consistency of whipped cream. It was then poured into a flat tray or box and the carved compo or wood patterns pressed down into it,

working them a little from side to side to make sure the compo fitted close and to remove air bubbles. When the compo had set hard the patterns were removed and the mould coated with black lead which made it easier to remove the decorations to be cast in it.

Alternatively the carver worked a reverse pattern in wood, into which the compo could be poured, but this was a difficult and tedious job and was only used when there was a large amount of repetitive work to do, or when the mould was likely to be stored for use at a future date.

The same compo mixture was used to make the copies. It was poured carefully into the mould and at the same time the mould was agitated with a small stick to make sure it entered all the details of the carving and was free of air bubbles. When the copies had set and were removed from the mould they were coated with resin solution. It will be appreciated that this type of moulding could not have any undercut or it would not have released from the mould, so all the undercutting had to be worked by hand afterwards.

Fortunately for the restorer, there is now on the market a synthetic rubber known as Vinamould which can be used instead of the compo mould and which will allow for the undercut as well. Enclose the moulded decoration which is to be copied in a wood frame, the sides of which are approximately $\frac{1}{4}$in higher than the highest part of the decoration. The synthetic rubber is heated until it is liquid and poured into the box frame, filling it completely. When it has set, the frame can be removed and the rubber peeled off the decoration. It is then replaced in the wood frame which will keep it in its true shape. The normal compo mixture can be used in this mould to make copies of the decoration. There is no danger of either the original or the compo sticking to the mould.

GESSO

This was probably used originally as a grain filler when a surface was required which was flat and even; but it was found that by putting a layer on top of the surface it could be rubbed down and levelled to an almost metallic finish which gave a more suitable surface for applying gold leaf or lacquer than that which was achieved by just filling the grain.

The mixture is composed of whitening, animal glue size, and a little raw linseed oil which makes it easier to apply. It should only be mixed as required because it will not keep in workable condition for any length of time. Put the whitening in a mortar and grind it with the pestle to remove any lumps and to get it fine and even. If only a small quantity is required it may be ground on a tile or glass palette with a palette-knife or thin-bladed dinner knife. When the whitening is ground even, cold water is added to it, stirring all the time until a consistency of whipped cream is reached. Heat the animal glue to the consistency which would be necessary for gluing joints, that is to say, just thin enough to run off the brush without hanging to it like treacle. Add this to the whitening until the mixture has a consistency of cream. To this add one desertspoon of raw linseed oil to every half pint of the liquid.

Gesso is applied with a brush like paint, but there is no need to wait for one layer to dry out before applying another. It is applied layer on layer until the required thickness is reached and then it is left to dry out completely. The levelling off of the new gesso to the level of the original should be done first with square-edge scrapers, then rubbed over lightly with glass, garnet or silicone paper and finally with a cloth damped with water. This last operation is most important because it removes any loose pigment and also burnishes the surface.

PAINTED SURFACES

Modern oil paint should not be used for restoring damaged paint surfaces because it is not possible to match the old surface finishes with an oil paint, but emulsion paint may be used on large background surfaces.

If there is coloured floral or other decoration which needs restoration, mix dry pigment colours with genuine turpentine to a consistency of whipped cream, and then add gilding quality gold size until it is cream consistency, and apply with a paint brush. After all coloured decoration is completed it should be rubbed down with silicone paper or 0000 gauge wire wool, and wiped with a damp cloth before giving it a thin coat of transparent button polish.

Dry Pigment Colours
Red lead is used for colouring grain filler and is used with glue size for colouring cabinet backs and interiors, and also with thinned button shellac for toning down rich mahogany colour when touching up repair work. It is used under gold and also for lacquer repairs.

Lemon chrome is used for touching up painted decoration and is mixed with red or blue to obtain orange or green colours. It can be used in filler for satinwood and other light yellow timbers. It can also be used to tone down rich colours when touching up repairs on polished furniture, for lacquer repairs and under gold leaf.

Orange chrome can be used for similar purposes to red lead and lemon chrome.

Turkey or burnt umber is sometimes needed for paint restoration, it is used in filler, but its main use is for toning in backgrounds of gilded, painted or polished furniture to match original areas where dust has collected, the surface is first waxed and burnished, and the pigment colour is then dusted on dry with a soft brush and it will cling to the wax in the background.

The greenish tint in this pigment makes it match the original dust very closely.

Ivory, lamp or gas black is used in beeswax polish to avoid it showing as light flecks in the grain of the wood, it is also used for toning polished repairs, and for colouring gesso and lacquer.

Titanium white is used for touching up painted work and lacquer, it is also occasionally required for polished repair colouring.

Prussian blue is used for painted work and also for lacquer.

Rose pink is used in mahogany filler.

Any of these colours can be mixed together to obtain a particular shade and no other colours should be necessary.

GILDING

Oil gilding
Under no circumstances should gold paint (bronze powder mixed with either oil size or spirit size) be used for restoring areas where gold is missing, because over a very short time it will turn a dark brown-green colour. For restoring small areas of missing gold, first make sure that the gesso surface is perfect, if not build it up again with new gesso. Then apply 4-6 hour gilding quality gold size to the surfaces, taking into account that it will need 2-3 hours to dry back ready for gilding and will only stay at that stage for about 2-3 hours more. In other words, do no more than can be covered with the gold leaf before it dries out too far.

There is usually a colour under the gold and this should be matched accurately (red, orange, yellow or sometimes, on Victorian furniture, black). With the oil gilding this colour is best applied as a separate coat on top of the gesso before applying the gold size. It should be rubbed down with silicone paper or 000 gauge wire wool and wiped over with a damp cloth.

Small areas of missing gold are probably best replaced by using transfer gold leaf, pressed into position with upholsterer's wadding or the fingers, because it is easier to distress and match up to the original. If the gold is fairly highly burnished it will be necessary to put on a second layer of gold and this can be done by applying beeswax polish (see page 97 on mixing beeswax polish) over the surface and burnishing it. The second layer of gold is then applied immediately and burnished with a soft brush. The distressing can be done either with the same brush or, if it is excessive, it can be done with a fine crocus powder on a soft cloth which has been damped with raw linseed oil. Before using the powder, the gold size must be left for at least 24 hours to dry out. After all gilding repairs are completed, the whole of the gold surface, the new and the old, should be polished with beeswax which will act as a protection against further damage and also stops further deterioration of the original gold. This should be done carefully, coating a small area at a time with wax and burnishing immediately. If the soft wax is left on too long it may release the gold.

If large areas need to be gilded then it will probably be necessary to use the loose leaf gold instead of the transfer leaf, and for this process special tools and equipment are needed, namely a gilder's cushion, tip, and knife, Fig. 127. The cushion is a board approximately 6in × 8in padded on the face side with two or three layers of felt covered with suede leather which is pulled firmly over the felt, and fixed round the edges to the back of the board. The tip is a kind of brush made with a piece of fine cardboard folded in two with a thin layer of firm hair glued along the inside edge of the opening edge of the fold. The knife is straight-bladed and is used for cutting up the gold on the cushion, so the edge, though fine, must not be sharp enough to cut the suede leather. It is necessary to put a screen, made of parchment or strong brown paper standing 4in high, along one end of the cushion and half way down the two sides. This prevents the gold being blown off it, which can happen with even the slightest draught.

When loose leaf gilding it is advisable, if possible,

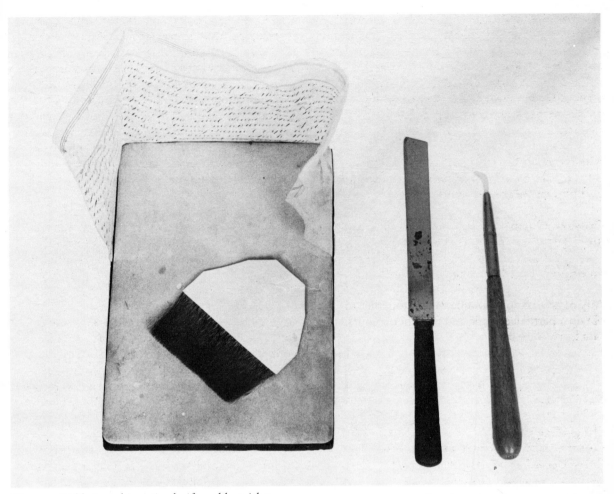

Fig. 127 Gilder's cushion, tip, knife and burnisher.

to do it in a draught-free room where people are not continually moving past because the gold is so light that the slightest wind will blow it off the pad and it is very difficult to retrieve, which could prove very costly. The tip is first magnetised by running the hair on it through the hair on the head of the restorer. It is then laid on the edge of a leaf of the gold which is lifted and laid on the cushion. If it is not lying perfectly flat give a short sharp puff of wind on the centre of the leaf to lay it flat. It can then be cut with the knife into convenient sizes for laying. Pick up the piece to be used with the magnetised tip and lay it on the surface to be gilded, again blow on it to make sure that it is lying true on the gold size. Cover the whole surface to be gilded before any surplus gold is dusted off. (This surplus gold can be saved by the gilder and sold.) The disadvantage of oil gilding is that it cannot be highly burnished as it can on water gilding.

Water gilding

The gesso preparation for water gilding is the same as that for oil gilding, but on top of the gesso is put a layer of bole. This resembles clay, and consists essentially of silica, alumina, and oxide of iron and is mixed with rabbit-skin glue size to a creamy consistency. It is painted over the gesso, applying a number of coats, and when it is dry it is rubbed down and levelled in the same way as the gesso. When water gilding it is best if the surface being gilded is laid at an angle so that the surplus water will run off. Coat only the area which the leaf or piece of leaf will cover liberally with cold water applied with a camel-hair or similar brush. The gold leaf is immediately floated on top of it, the surplus water will run away from beneath it and the rabbit-skin glue will soften enough for the leaf to adhere to it.

Where very high burnishing is required a second layer of gold leaf should be applied with water in the same way as the first layer. When all surfaces have been gilded they should be left to set before burnishing. This is done with an agate fixed in a pencil-like tool which is lightly lubricated with wax and rubbed over the surface of the gilt until the required shine is achieved. A disadvantage when restoring with water gilt is that the water is liable to loosen and destroy the original gilding so great care should be taken when working with it. A thin layer of wax polish over the original gilt will help to prevent this. The bole used under the water gilding has a cushioning effect and when the agate is being used there is less danger of the gold being torn than there would be if the gold was directly on to the gesso. The distressing of water gilding is done by the same method as for oil gilt, using fine crocus or silicone powder on a soft cloth damped with raw linseed oil.

RESTORATION AND CONSERVATION OF LACQUER

Restoring lacquer surfaces is painstaking and difficult if a first class result is to be achieved, and it is best to practise on articles of little or no value before attempting a valuable piece.

There are two kinds of flat lacquer; English lacquer which has a layer of gesso beneath the surface finish and Chinese and Japanese lacquers which are applied directly on to the surface of the timber. There is also bantam work which is lacquer with raised and incised surfaces. Chinese lacquer is the highest quality and usually only seen on valuable pieces of furniture. Japanese lacquer is poorer in quality with very little thickness or body to it, and is found on pieces of less valuable furniture and on papier-mâché articles. English lacquer is usually found on pieces of furniture of typically European design, and is easily identified by the white gesso which is sure to show somewhere.

One of the main faults with old lacquer is that the surfaces crackle and the edges round the cracks release and lift. These can be re-laid by coating the whole surface with a thin layer of beeswax polish and then, with a tightly-rolled pad of well-washed cotton cloth (not a wadding-filled french polish pad) soaked with methylated spirits, go over the surface with a circular action, first very lightly and then as the lacquer begins to re-lay the pressure can be increased. If any of the design shows signs of moving then leave it for a period and work on another part. With perseverance the lacquer will usually lie completely flat again and the cracks will be filled with the wax which is hardened by the methylated spirits. The levelling and the filling of the cracks is the first operation and should be done before any other lacquer repairs are done.

When restoring small areas of missing lacquer the author has found from experience that if the true gum-lac is used it shrinks and leaves a gap where the new meets the old; it also tends to crack and break away the edges of the old lacquer. If a solution made up of colour pigment, oil gold size and turpentine (for mixing see page 85) is layered on to the damaged surface until it is a little above the surface of the old and then left to dry thoroughly, it will look and work the same as the lacquer but will not shrink away at the edges. The levelling off of the new surface should be done with square-edged scrapers and finished with fine garnet or silicone paper or, if preferred, oooo gauge wire wool, finally wiped with a damp cloth and burnished with a dry one.

All the colour decoration can be restored with the gold size mixture paint. Gold leaf should be applied on oil gold size into which has been mixed a little lemon chrome pigment. Silver leaf should be laid on with gold size into which a little light blue (prussian blue) and titanium white has been mixed. On the Chinese lacquered furniture gold leaf is usually found under the red and yellow decoration, and silver under the blue and white decoration. It is necessary, if any of this is missing, to replace it, otherwise a true colour match will not be achieved.

Damaged bantam work can be built up with gesso

(whitening and animal glue) to which should be added colour pigments to match it to the original. These should be added at the first stage of mixing, when only water has been added, before the glue is mixed in. It is applied by brush in layers until it is a little over the correct thickness and when it is hard it can be carved and shaped with carving tools. It should then be wiped over with a damp cloth and coated with matching colour oil gold size paint, and finally wax polished. (For mixing gold size paint and gesso see page 85.)

GRAINING

The technique of graining was used from about the beginning of the 17th century when inferior woods were used for construction and the grain of the more expensive woods copied in paint on top.

The original graining was done with a distemper. The background colour is a mixture of white lead, linseed oil and rotten-stone (decomposed limestone) and/or venetian red, depending whether it is for oak, walnut or mahogany. These pigments and the oil are mixed with thin animal glue size applied with a brush and allowed to dry before rubbing down and levelling. The graining coat is then applied using the same sort of mixture but, of course, adjusting the colour for the darker shades in the woods. When the coat of colour is tacky a comb is used on it to mark in the grain. The combs were made from thin springy steel with cut outs along one edge similar to a hair comb. The figure is marked in by taking a piece of thin soft rag or leather, placing it over the thumb of the hand, two or three layers in thickness, and marking in the figure and medullary rays with the thumb nail. Finally the surface is wiped over with a soft brush made from camel-hair or similar to soften the edges of the figure marks, and when dry coated with one or two coats of varnish.

MARBLING

This is done by first applying a mixture of pigment colours the same as for the graining background. The top colours are mixed with half-and-half oil gold size and turpentine. The various colours are dabbed on with a brush or cloth and blended into each other and a fine pencil brush is used to put in the thin lines. The whole is finally coated with varnish.

SCAGLIOLA

This is a composition made by mixing plaster of Paris and glue size and adding pieces of fibrous gypsum, marble, alabaster and porphyry (a purple and white rock), etc. It was often applied on to a slate bed and the surface ground down with sandstone and pumicestone until flat, and then burnished and rubbed over with linseed oil. It was also made up into floral designs.

Restoring surface finishes

Colouring and surface finishing is the most important technique in furniture restoration. The skill used in making perfect woodwork repairs can be completely nullified by careless or unskilled colouring and finishing. First the surface finish on the new timber must be correct before any staining or colouring is commenced. It should be damped over with water to make certain there is no lifting of the wood grain. If it does lift it should be rubbed down with fine garnet or glasspaper using very little pressure. The surface must be allowed to dry before starting to paper it, otherwise the operation is wasted because the grain will still rise again when it is stained.

The surface of an antique piece of furniture is covered with small bruises caused by years of wear and tear and this affects the light and shade of the colour. It cannot usually be seen with the naked eye but can be seen under a magnifying glass. An armour-burnisher, Fig. 128, made from a leather square with linked chain fixed over its surface, held in the flat of the hand and tapped carefully over the wood surface will obtain this slight bruising which is necessary for the colouring to be accurate.

FUMING

This was originally done by putting the furniture in an airtight box or room with trays of ammonia. In even earlier days it was put in the horse stable or covered with horse manure, and the ammonia in the manure acted as a fume. When oak has been fumed the medullary rays are dark brown in colour, when unfumed the rays are lighter than the background. Because ammonia is also a paint and polish stripper, which continued to be used by some of the older polishers up to the early 1930's, it would be unwise to fume new parts by placing them in a fume box which might affect the original polish. Instead, the ammonia is applied directly on to the surface to be fumed. Very little is needed and it can be applied with a cloth. If a brush is used the ammonia will damage the hair or bristle. Full-strength commercial ammonia (.880) should be used and the fuming action can be stopped at any time, when it is felt that the depth of colour is right, by washing it liberally with water. Washing soda (not caustic soda which damages the surface finish and affects the cellular construction of the timber) can also be used for fuming. It is applied in the same way as the ammonia and gives a richer colour. It too must be neutralised with water.

STAINS

Vandyke–crystal water stain

This is made by pouring boiling water over the crystals and stirring thoroughly and then allowing to stand until it is cold. A tablespoon of ammonia added to each pint of liquid will help to make it strike deeper into the grain. If ammonia is added, the stain should be kept in an airtight container, preferably not metal because the stain will eat into it. By pouring boiling water over a quantity of the crystal the stain can be made to full strength (approximately one gallon to half a pound of crystals) and any

Fig. 128 Chain armour burnisher.

surplus crystal which will not suspend in the water will sink to the bottom and can be used later by pouring more boiling water on to it. If the stain is not required at full strength it can be removed from the main container and thinned down with cold water.

Vandyke stain should be applied liberally over the surfaces, preferably with a piece of hessian (burlap) or a brush and dried off with another hessian cloth. When dry it should be coated with a thin button shellac (four parts of spirits to one part of shellac), because it is not a dye, but more like a pigment stain. If, for example, wax polish was applied directly on to it, the colour might be released and would finish uneven. If a very dark brown is required this can be obtained by adding animal glue to the vandyke stain (about one tablespoon of ready-mixed animal glue to the pint). With lamp black added to it, Vandyke stain is used as an undercoat for ebonised finish. Vandyke stain is the most useful of all the stains and is a must for the restorer to have. Some polishers do not care for it because of the danger of the water lifting the grain but if the timber surface is prepared correctly by damping and rubbing down there should be no difficulty.

Potassium bichromate

This is usually known as chrome in the trade and although mixed with water has an action similar to a fume. When first applied there is only a slight yellowing of the timber but as it dries so the colour enriches until, if used at full strength, it will turn the timber surface almost black.

The chrome is prepared by adding a little of the crystal at a time to boiling water and stirring it until it dissolves. For full-strength solution, one ounce of crystal to a pint of water should suffice. It is advisable to first mix the chrome to full strength and then add cold water until, by testing on a sample of the same timber, the correct shade of colour is reached. It is essential to take great care when matching the colour because it cannot be washed off like an ordinary water or oil stain. If the colour is wrong it can only be removed by using a scraper. Chrome was mainly used from the early part of the 18th century for colouring mahogany but was also occasionally used on oak when a red tint was required, normally over-stained with Vandyke. It is stated to have been used on walnut but when this was tested it was found to have very little effect on most walnuts.

Bicarbonate of soda

Similar in its action to chrome and particularly effective on walnut.

Potassium permanganate

Used occasionally for colouring, the mixing and action is similar to chrome, but the colour finish is purple rather than red.

Red oil

Raw linseed oil dyed by putting alkanet root into it which turns the oil a rich red colour. It was used for colouring walnut and mahogany and appears to have been used from early in the 17th century.

Oil and naphthalene stains

These are easier to use than the fumes and water stains, but they are not really suitable for restoration work because they fade and alter colour in a fairly short period of time, and thus show up rather badly any patch repairs which have been coloured with them.

Mineral and vegetable dyes

These were used mainly for colouring inlays and veneers and this applies particularly to some of the veneers used for marquetry. They are now used for adjusting patch repairs when the staining does not match the colour required perfectly. For this purpose the dye is mixed with thin shellac polish.

Black is used to tone down and darken red. It can also be used to simulate ebony by boiling sycamore or pear veneers in water to which the black dye had been added. Stringing (line inlay) was also done by this method.

Bismarke brown is not really a brown, it is a rich red dye and used in thin shellac polish to enrich small areas. It is sometimes used mixed in the coating shellac for a whole surface but should be used very carefully, making sure that each stroke of the brush does not overlap the previous stroke, or it will finish very patchy. It is also used for dyeing veneers.

Aniline green is used for dyeing the green leaves in marquetry. It is also used in thin shellac polish for reducing the red and slightly darkening rich colours. It should be used with great restraint or the surfaces will finish with a green tint.

Crysodine is an orange dye which is most useful to the restorer because it obtains the honey tone on walnut and mahogany which dealers are so fond of, it is mixed in thin shellac polish.

Alcavar orange is similar to crysodine and used for the same purpose, but is slightly more yellow.

Spirit yellow in thin shellac polish is used where a rich colour needs to be reduced and made lighter.

Magenta is used in thin shellac polish and has the effect of darkening a red colour but must be used with great restraint or it will show purple.

Turmeric is not a true dye (it is used in green pickles to enrich the colour and can be obtained from most chemists) but it is used, after the initial coating of shellac, to reduce richness and

is mixed with thin shellac polish. The effect is similar to chrome where the change of colour is not immediate but comes gradually as it dries. Practice is required in its use but once it is mastered it can be an asset to the restorer.

Oxide of iron was used to dye sycamore which gave a silver-grey colour with a slight tint of green, called harewood, but over a period of time the green becomes much more pronounced.

Verdigris in a solution of acetic acid (vinegar) was used to dye sycamore green for leaves, etc., for marquetry, and can still be used if desired.

All dyes mixed with spirit and shellac will fade, so they should only be used as a last resort.

GRAIN FILLERS

The original grain filler was a mixture of whitening, genuine turpentine, and raw linseed oil. Three parts of turpentine to one part of linseed oil was prepared and fine-ground whitening was added until a consistency of whipped cream was obtained. Tallow was sometimes included in the mixture, one large dessertspoon to each pint. The filler was applied with a piece of hessian (burlap) using a circular action. It was then allowed to dry off until it appeared dull and powdery and then the surplus on the surface was removed with a piece of clean dry hessian (burlap), and finally brushed over with a soft brush to remove any loose pigment.

Although the filler was sometimes used in its white state for some of the lighter woods, it was more often coloured with pigments to match the colour of the timber; rose pink and brown umber for mahogany, yellow ochre, brown umber and raw sienna for oak and walnut and these were added immediately after the whitening. A disadvantage with this grain filler was that the pigment colours sucked back into the whitening leaving a white fleck in the grain, although this is not so pronounced when tallow has been included. The whitening fleck is most often seen in the later Victorian period when African mahogany was in use and should not be confused with the white fleck in Cuban mahogany which is natural in the growth of the tree. Polishing suppliers now have a patent grain filler which the restorer can use. It is much cleaner to use, dries quickly and if the restorer buys the natural pigment, colours can be added to just the quantity required for a particular job, saving time and expense.

HOLE STOPPERS

These vary considerably depending on the purpose for which they are going to be used. If timber is split or damaged and cannot be filled with a wood skiver, a fine dust of the same timber mixed with enough glue size to just hold it together, not made into a soft paste or it will shrink and work loose, should be forced into the damaged area. When hard it can be worked level and to shape with chisels or a plane. It will stain, colour and polish the same as timber.

For small pin and nail holes, wax and resin (3 of wax to 1 of resin) can be melted over a flame and dry pigments added to obtain the right colour. If this is then poured on to cold water it can be picked off again almost immediately and rolled with the hands into a stick. It is best applied with a knife, not melted in because it shrinks as it hardens again. This will take polish but will not stain so that colour must be accurate. If there is a slight variation it can be adjusted with spirit colour in thin shellac polish.

A paste stopper made of china clay mixed with glue size, to which pigment colours are added to get the correct shade, is an alternative to the wax stopper and there is very little shrinkage after applying it.

STRIPPING AND CLEANING POLISHED SURFACES

Polished surfaces should never be stripped unless it is certain that the finish is not original. The patina, as the old surface is called, can usually be conserved and to remove it completely can devalue a piece of furniture by at least a third.

Patina is only achieved by hundreds of years of loving care and attention and is the result of continual dusting and polishing together with exposure to bright light. Shellac was used on furniture from around 1700, but a certain amount was gradually removed again by the continual abrasive action of the furniture being dusted, on top of this was built up a layer of wax polish from which the natural oil, over this long period of time, had gradually dried out leaving the wax probably as hard as the french polish shellac finish (which was used in England from around 1820) and this patina resists water and spirit being spilt on it better than french polish.

Before anything is done to the surface finish, all repairs should be completed, no matter how poor and dirty it may be as a result of neglect. The dust and dirt which has collected on the furniture will have affected the colour of the original finish, and this dust and dirt spreading on to the new surfaces when the furniture is cleaned will help to adjust and match them to the original. If a piece of furniture is reasonably clean but still not quite good enough for the final finishing, wipe over with a cloth soaked in warm soapy water. Alternatively use vinegar and water instead of soap, particularly if the surface appears to be very greasy. This will remove the grease and also harden the surface to a certain extent.

If the surface is gilded under no circumstances should water be used to clean it or the gold will lift off and the surface will be destroyed. Methylated spirits may be used with great care instead, brushing on and wiping off a small area at a time using a soft cloth. If the gold shows any sign of moving, the spirit should be patted off and the area left to dry out before any further cleaning is attempted. It is fairly common to find gold surfaces painted over with bronze powder (gold paint) and this should be removed. This was usually done because the leaf gold underneath was in poor condition and after attempting to touch it up with gold paint it was found impossible to match, and so the whole surface had been coated with bronze powder. The gold paint will discolour over a very short period and turn a dark browny-green, almost black, which is sometimes mistaken for an original dark brown pigment colour. To strip this gold paint (bronze powder in gold size) the author has found that Nitro-mors Original (not the water washable Nitro-mors) can be used if methylated spirits will not remove it, but it must be used with even greater care than when stripping with spirit. The stripper is brushed on to a small surface area and worked around with the soft brush until the paint shows signs of moving. It should then be patted off, not rubbed, with a soft cloth. When the whole area has been treated in this way it can usually be further improved by washing over carefully with methylated spirits. The surface must be allowed to thoroughly dry out before any missing gold leaf is replaced.

A false finish of french polish on top of an original finish is usually the result of a french polisher who has no restoring experience, being asked to brighten up a piece of furniture. He does so by rubbing it over two or three times with a french polish rubber thus coating it with a thin layer of button shellac. This will not last for any length of time, as it soon begins to show a yellow tint and often starts to crackle. It can usually be fairly easily removed with methylated spirit applied with a brush on a small area at a time and wiped off with a soft cotton cloth. When the whole area has been treated in this way it should be spirited-out in exactly the same way as the polisher would spirit-out a french polish surface (see page 98 on french polishing).

A very dirty original surface can be cleaned with a weak solution of washing soda in warm water (2 ounces of soda to a gallon of water) but before using this any new unpolished areas must be coated with button shellac otherwise the soda will fume and alter their colour. After washing with the soda and water, and if the surface is then reasonably bright, it can be washed over with clear water and burnished with a cloth. If it is dull it can be worked over with a spirit pad in the same way as spiriting-out when french polishing.

Cleaning painted surfaces can usually be done with either warm soapy water or with the weak solution of washing soda and water, but if the soda and water is used, only a small area should be done at a time and if there is any sign of the paint softening it should be washed over with clear water and left to dry before any further cleaning is done to that area. When a surface has been cleaned with soda and water it should always be washed over with clear water. A little soap or, for preference, domestic washing-up liquid may be added to the water if it is felt that it will improve the finish.

If lacquered surfaces need cleaning it should be done with a thin beeswax and turpentine solution applied with a brush over a small area at a time and wiped off with a soft cotton cloth. If the decoration shows any sign of moving the area should be left until the wax has hardened and it should then be burnished with a clean dry brush or cloth.

REMOVING FALSE FINISHES

Fortunately it is only very occasionally that a piece of antique furniture has been stripped completely and re-polished, and usually this has been done by the french polish method which has a hard appearance with the polish showing as a layer on top of the wood surface, rather than the wood face itself being polished. If in doubt about the finish test it by laying one hand flat on the surface and laying the other hand on a french polish finish, if the french polish finish feels much colder then the possibility is that the other is original. Another method is to put a drop of methylated spirit on to an area where it will be least noticeable and if it starts to soften the surface immediately then it is likely to be a french polish finish. It should be pointed out, however, that the french polishing method was used widely from the beginning of the Victorian period so most Victorian furniture would have been french polished originally.

When it is evident that a finish is not original it should be stripped off carefully with Nitro-mors Original or a similar mild stripper, using a wallpaper stripper to remove the softened polish, taking care not to scrape or scratch the surface of the timber which would show as a dis-coloured patch. After the bulk of the polish has been removed the surface can be finally cleaned by rubbing it over with fine 000-0000 gauge wire wool soaked in methylated spirit, drying it off with a clean cotton cloth. Caustic strippers should *never* be used for stripping antique furniture because they have a fuming effect and would alter the colour of the wood. Once the colour has been lost it is almost impossible to regain it. When the stripping has been completed the surfaces should be coated with thin shellac made up of 4 parts methylated spirit to 1 part of button shellac. Rub down lightly with flour grade glasspaper or an equivalent garnet or silicone paper, which has been coated with a thin film of linseed oil to stop the shellac building up on it and causing scratches on the wood surface. Any loose dust should be removed with a cloth. slightly damped with water.

The colour should now be checked to make sure it is reasonably even, particularly where any new repair work has been done, and this should be adjusted if required with either pigment or spirit colours mixed in thin shellac and very lightly rubbed over with oiled flour paper or fine wire wool. A second coat of the thin button shellac should then be applied with a camel hair polisher's mop and lightly rubbed down again. It will then be ready for polishing which is dealt with on page 96.

False painted finishes can usually be easily recognised because they will be done with oil paints which have a hard shiny appearance, whereas the original, although coated with varnish, will have a powdery look. Also any protruding areas will probably show signs of chipping which will expose the original paint, polish or gold beneath. If there is any doubt, however, a small area should be dry stripped using a round-edged copper or brass scraper.

The false coat will usually strip off fairly easily, as it does not normally adhere very strongly to the original finish. Having found that the finish is false, often the easiest and best way to strip it is to remove it dry, using the round-edged copper or brass scraper. Though this is rather tedious it is not difficult and can be done by an apprentice, if shown how. If the finish will not

dry strip, then a non-caustic stripper (Nitro-mors Original) should be used, work on a small area at a time using a very thin coat of the stripper and agitating it with the brush until the paint shows signs of movement and then wiping it off clean with a dry cloth. When the complete surface has been stripped it should be washed carefully with clean soapy water. Normally there will be a certain amount of damage to the original finish and this should be restored as described on page 85. The old surfaces and the shellac surfaces should then be wax polished, but the painted original surface should first be coated with thin transparent button shellac before waxing it.

POLISHES AND POLISHING

Wax polishes were the earliest polishes to be used, before then the surfaces were just finished by oiling with a vegetable oil.

Very early pieces of furniture were just rubbed over with the block of beeswax and levelled off with either a cork or softwood rubber which was not very satisfactory because it left the finish rather uneven. Later the beeswax was dissolved in turpentine and applied as a paste which was much more satisfactory. A number of coats were needed to build up a reasonable surface polish and each coat had to be left for a period of time to dry out, otherwise a layer on top would just soften the layers beneath and cause the whole finish to be uneven. Varnish was also used on some of the early furniture and continued to be used into the early mahogany period. The early varnish was not very satisfactory because it tended to crackle but later beeswax was added to it and this was better but still not perfect. It was not until 1820 when the french polishing method was brought into this country that a really smooth and satisfactory shellac finish was achieved. There are three types of shellac, seed, flake and button, and the only suitable one for furniture polishing is the button. The others will produce a cloudy finish at best. It is really uneconomic to make up your own shellac polish, it is better to go to a reliable paint and polish supplier to obtain good quality button shellac polish.

Fig. 129 Preparing a wax polish rubber.

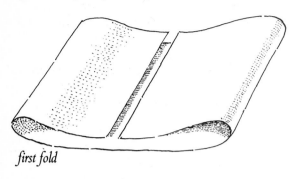

first fold

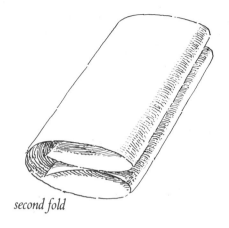

second fold

these folds are repeated with the opposite edges.

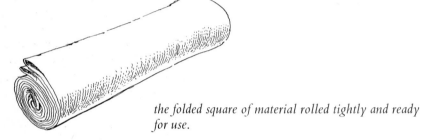

the folded square of material rolled tightly and ready for use.

A very good hard polish finish for mahogany and walnut, which dates back to around the beginning of the walnut period, is referred to by Sheraton in his Cabinet Dictionary, and this was certainly used up to the early 1930's. The author himself has used it on surfaces such as bar and bank counters where it had to stand up to a terrific amount of wear and tear. The timber surface was first coated with raw linseed oil and then, if on walnut, tripoly powder (decomposed limestone), or if on mahogany, brick-dust (powdered red clay) was scattered over the surface. Using about a half-hundredweight weight covered with felt or similar material, the surface was worked over, forcing the powder into the grain and also mixing it with the oil, until a hard polish finish was achieved. This was a long, hard, tedious job which took so many man-hours that it could only be used on the best and most expensive furniture but when it was finished it was almost indestructable. This type of finishing went out of use when the cellulose spray finishes came into use, and these have now been outdated by the synthetic resins such as polyurethane and polyester lacquers.

WAX POLISHING

In the early days a good wax polish could only be achieved by waiting a long period of time between each coat. The author has found by trial and error over the years, that this waiting between coats could be almost completely overcome by spiriting-out each coat with methylated spirit in a similar way that the french polisher spirits-out the shellac. The pad should not be filled with wadding as for french polish but is best made from a square of well-washed cotton cloth about three spans of the hand in size. Two opposite edges of the cloth are folded over to meet each other at the centre. One half is then folded again to completely cover the other half, the other two edges are then folded to meet each other in the centre and folded in half again. The cloth is rolled tightly, Fig. 129, and is ready for use.

Beeswax is used and it should first be flaked with a sharp knife or chisel and put into a glass or earthenware container which should be filled to the brim. Genuine turpentine is then poured on to just cover the wax. The wax will begin to dissolve as the turps is poured and will probably finish up by filling only about three-quarters of the container. A salt-spoonful of lamp, gas or ivory black should then be added to each pound or pint of the mixture and the whole thoroughly stirred. The mixture should not be heated to speed up the melting of the wax because this will make the wax sticky, leave to dissolve on its own, occasionally giving it a stir. It will be ready for use in about four to six hours.

Grip the firmly-rolled (this is most important) pad lengthways in one hand, one end to the finger tips and the other towards the wrist. Holding one end of the pad with the finger tips, press the other end of the pad into the palm of the hand with the other hand. The underside of the pad should be convex in its length and is now ready for use. Smear a layer of the beeswax on to the face of the pad, and using a circular action apply the wax on to the timber surface, using a fair amount of pressure to force it into the grain and spreading it as far as it will go. Repeat the operation until the grain is nicely filled and the surface has a nice even layer of wax over it. Now stroke the pad firmly *across* the grain over the full length of the surface, and repeat the operation but this time *with* the grain. Any surplus wax will now be at the outside edges of the timber and can be removed with the fingers.

The pad should now be well soaked with methylated spirit, but not dripping wet, and with a small circular action, work over the face of the wax fairly firmly along the length of the grain. Start at the edge furthest away and work gradually towards the near edge, overlapping each line of circles on to the previous one. Continue this operation until a dry shine is following the rubber (the spirit is quickly drying out and the wax is shining) then with the rubber still moist, work with straight strokes across the grain over the full length, and then, stroking with the grain and starting at the edge furthest

away, work with straight strokes gradually towards the near edge. Continue with this, reducing the pressure a little each time the rubber is moved again to the far edge, also each time the rubber is moved to the far edge the stroke should be started at the opposite end to the previous starting end. This should be continued until the surface is free of rubber streaks.

A second thin layer of wax can be put evenly and immediately over the surface with the rubber. Wipe the rubber over with the hand to remove surplus wax and then soak the rubber with methylated spirit and repeat the previous operation starting with the circular action. It is not necessary to press quite so firmly this time. This surface finish will come very quickly and then a third layer of wax can be put on. Up to four layers of wax can be applied which should give a good high gloss finish. If more layers are put on, there is a danger of the surface having an orange-peel effect. Although the surface is now reasonably hard and shiny, it will be about a week before it is really hard and if the furniture is going to be delivered before that, the customer should be advised to not put anything on top of it for a week. If these instructions are not followed and the top is marked, it can only be removed by the restorer using methylated spirits. The customer should also be advised not to use furniture cream on it for at least six months, but only to polish it with a soft duster.

Wax polishing new patch repairs
When new pieces of timber have been fitted into a surface and they have been colour matched they should first be coated with thin button shellac, then with a finger they can be coated with wax making sure the grain is filled and that there is a fairly thick even layer on the surface. It should be left to harden for about twenty-four hours and then completely hardened off with the methylated spirit pad. The restorer should not concentrate on the patches, but move evenly over the whole surface using the circular rubbing action which releases a little of the original wax and spreads it on to the new surfaces thus improving the finish. When the

outline of the wax on the new patches has disappeared the surface can be straightened off, first once across the grain, and then with the grain until streaks are removed.

If there is a very thick layer of wax on a surface which has had new pieces fitted into it it is sometimes preferable to rub the block of wax on it when coating the new patches, this will particularly apply to early oak furniture when the wax will be uneven anyway. It should then be hardened and levelled off with the methylated spirit pad, again working over the whole surface.

Badly bruised surfaces
If a surface into which new pieces have been fitted, is very badly bruised the new areas should be matched to the old with the armour-burnisher, Fig. 127, after the first wax has been applied but before any spiriting-out is done.

On carving, legs, etc., the wax can be applied with a brush and then spirited out with the pad.

FRENCH POLISHING

To make the rubber take about a 12in square of well-washed cotton cloth and about a 10in square of upholsterer's grey wadding (do not use cotton wool because it goes hard when soaked in the polish). Fold up the wadding by folding the outside edges inwards until it is formed into a small round-faced pad with a point at one end of it; the skin of the wadding should be to the outside. Soak the wadding with the button polish and place it in the centre of the cotton cloth. Hold the pad in the palm of one hand and with the other hand take the edge of the cloth which is opposite the pad point and start twisting it. It will gradually twist down until the point on the pad is held firmly. Carry on twisting until all edges are gathered in the twist and all the pad is held firmly in the cloth. The pad is now ready to use and should be stored in an air-tight container, Fig. 130.

Before using the pad apply two or three thin coats of button shellac with a good polisher's mop of camel or similar hair to the surfaces.

Fig. 130 Preparing a french polish rubber.

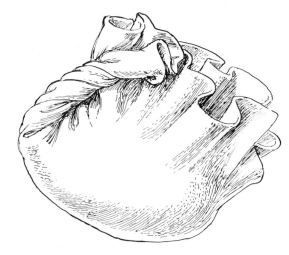

starting to twist.

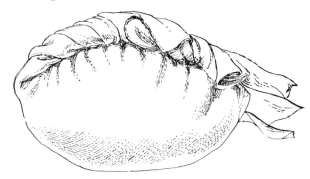

twist as it should lie on top of completed rubber.

They should then be rubbed down and levelled with fine garnet or silicone paper which has been coated with a thin layer of linseed oil to stop the shellac sticking to it and causing scratches. If the original surfaces are badly bruised the new areas should now be matched to them by using the armour-burnisher.

The pad can now be charged by dipping it into the polish. It is not necessary to remove the pad from the cloth when charging it but all surplus polish must be removed with the hand from the surface of the cloth or it will make an uneven finish. With a finger put a thin film of raw linseed oil on to the face of the pad to lubricate it and to stop it sticking to the polished surfaces. The building up of the polish can now commence, using either a circular action the same as for wax finishing or a figure of eight action, whichever is preferred. The main thing is that the whole surface is worked over evenly. There is a saying by polishers in the trade 'take care of the edges, the centre will take care of itself', and it is the edges which are likely to miss some of the bodying-up if the polisher is not very careful. Each time the rubber is charged with polish the surface of the rubber should also be skimmed over with linseed oil. When the polished surfaces have sufficient body on them they should then be straightened off, to remove any rubber marks. First once across the grain and then with the grain until the surface is level. The work should now be left for 24 hours to allow oil to rise to the surface and also for the shellac to harden.

Spiriting-out
After 24 hours it will probably be noticeable that the surface has gone dull. This is caused by oil rising to the surface and to remove it is the most difficult part of french polishing. It is removed by going in straight lines over the surface working lightly with the grain with the rubber loaded with neat methylated spirit until all smears have disappeared. It is very easy to loosen the surface of the polish if this is not done with great care and the rubber should only be well damped with the methylated spirit not soaked as it is for wax finishing.

French polishing new patches on old surfaces
The new surfaces should be built up with numerous coats of a mixture of half methylated spirit and half button polish, called half-and-half polish, which is applied with a polisher's camel-hair mop. Leave a few minutes drying time between each coat, working until the surface is slightly higher than the level of the original. When it is thoroughly hardened off after twenty-four hours it should be rubbed down and levelled with fine garnet or silicone paper coated with linseed oil, and then burnished with a soft cotton cloth to remove loose pigment and oil. A layer of wax should then be applied with a fingertip, spreading it as evenly as possible and making sure that it covers the surface of the new polish. After leaving it for a short time to allow the wax to settle down, the whole surface should be rubbed over with the wax polishing rubber moistened with methylated spirits. Start with a circular action and then straight across and finally with the grain, in the same way that a wax finish would be done. Wax previously applied to the old surface will then be spread over the new surfaces which should help to match them to each other, but do not concentrate on the new areas or the polish will be stripped off.

Dulling
Newly polished surfaces will be brighter than the old and it is necessary to dull them down but the surfaces must be really hard and dry before this is done. The dulling powder, crocus, charcoal or emery should be put in a cotton bag, and the powder applied by dabbing the bag over the surfaces. In this way no coarse pieces can get through to scratch the faces. With a soft bristle brush work the powder backwards and forwards, moving all the time *with* the grain and not across it, until it is dull enough and then sweep off the dust with the brush. Finally wipe over the surfaces with a soft cloth, again working with the grain, to make sure that all the powder has been removed. Restorers sometimes use glaziers putty on the surfaces to dull them instead of powder.

Bleaching
It is often necessary to apply bleach to lighten the colour of surfaces, particularly if the old surface finish has been disturbed a little when levelling off new pieces which have been fitted. For mild bleaching a solution of oxalic acid mixed with hot water will tone the wood down to a creamy colour. If a pale but warmer colour is required, hydrogen peroxide can be used. If a very mild bleaching is required oxalic acid mixed with methylated spirits may be used and this has the advantage of working and drying out very quickly. If a very strong bleaching is necessary then first coat the surface with ammonia and while it is still wet apply hydrogen peroxide, as soon as the wood has toned down to the correct colour the surface should be washed with water to neutralise the bleach. With this type of double-action bleaching it is not possible to bring back the colour again if it goes too light nor will it take a fume or stain very easily. All bleaching should be neutralised with water.

Upholstery

When the restorer removes the upholstery from a piece of furniture to do the woodwork repairs, he should always keep it as complete as possible in its original make-up so that even if it is rotten and cannot be used again, the upholsterer can see the style of the upholstery which came off, and can also, if necessary, take patterns from it. When stripping upholstery the tacks should always be ripped out with the grain not across it. An upholsterer must have a thorough knowledge of the development of upholstery techniques so that any missing upholstery can be replaced correct to period and style.

In the early 16th century upholstery work was mainly confined to beds and bedding, though a small number of cushions or pads were made to use on wood seat chairs. The covers were usually linen or canvas embroidered with needlework but velvet, damask, and satin were also used during this century. Sometimes leather was just stretched across the rails. Cushions were filled with feathers, down, hay or straw. Hair and wool were sometimes used but these were not considered to be very sanitary until about the middle of the century when special regulations came out which made sure they were more hygenic. Early mattresses for beds were supported by boring holes in the side and end rails and threading rope criss-cross between them. Alternatively, canvas or linen was stretched across and either fixed with rope looped through it and round the rails, or tacked to the rails. Towards the end of the 16th century upholstery began to play a much more important role, and beds in particular were covered and hung with elaborate floral needlework.

In the early part of the 17th century there was a rapid increase in the use of upholstery for decorative purposes as well as for comfort. Beds, in particular, were decorated with covered headboards, head curtains, pelmets, bedspreads and draw curtains. In the last quarter of the century the whole of the tester or canopy was often covered with ornate needlework or patterned velvet which was further ornamented with fringes, tassel trimming and decorative gimp and braid.

The tester was usually surmounted at the corners with material-covered finials with ostrich feathers sometimes used as part of the trimming. The bed posts were also covered with material instead of being carved. Chairs in the early part of the 17th century mainly had loose cushions laid on stretched linen or canvas which was fixed to the rails. The rails and the backs were covered with velvet, needlework or silk and in some cases the whole of the woodwork was covered, and like the beds was trimmed with fringes, tassles, gimps and braids. Brass dome-headed nails were often used to fix the trimmings. Stools were treated much in the same way, but the cushion was loosely stitched to the under-canvas.

From approximately 1620, seat furniture was made with fixed upholstery on the seats and backs. The stuffing was spread evenly over the stretched linen or canvas base and a second piece of linen or canvas was tacked over the top of it to keep it in place. The needlework, velvet or damask, was then fixed; usually in such a way that it could easily be removed for repairing or cleaning.

The dog or cock roll

It was not until about the middle of the 17th century that a stitched or tacked roll was used on top of the seat rails. This was made by allowing the base canvas to overhang the outside edge of the seat rails by approximately 3in. It was then folded back over the rails and the fold filled with hay or straw. The raw edge was then tucked in and either stitched to the canvas or tacked to the rail. Wool, hay, hair or straw was then spread between the rolls and linen or canvas fixed over it to hold it in place. This method of stuffing is still used for loose seats, Fig. 131.

Webbing appears to have come into use towards the end of the 17th century but it has not been possible to date it accurately.

Double stuffing

This came into use around the beginning of the 18th century but not in England until about 1730. Webbing is fixed on the top edge of the seat rails, a webbing width from the inside edge of the rails and approximately the same width apart. Canvas is then stretched over it and tacked down. The hair is then spread evenly on top of the canvas. Sometimes ties were used to hold the hair in place. These were loose loops of twine which were threaded through the canvas 3–4in from the edges, and if a large seat, a line of them was run through the centre, too. They were put in position before starting the stuffing and the hair was tucked under them. With the correct amount of stuffing in position, the canvas is temporarily tacked over the top and twine looped through it and down through the bottom canvas in a similar position to the lower hair ties and drawn tight enough to pull the top canvas down reasonably flat. The canvas is then fixed permanently. The raw edges are tucked in and tacked to the top edges of the rails. Sometimes the rails were bevelled off to receive the tacks.

The work will now be ready for stitching the edges and the number of rows of stitching depends on the height of the stuffing. A row of stitching should be allowed for each inch of height, for example, stuffing 3in above rails needs three rows of stitching. The lower rows of stitching are worked with a blind stitch; that

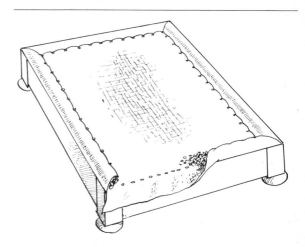

Fig. 131 Upholstery dog or cock roll.

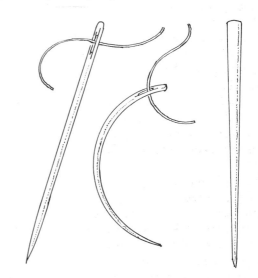

Fig. 132 Upholstery needles and regulator.

means that the stitches do not come through on to the top canvas. For this operation strong upholsterer's twine should be used and about an 8in long straight needle, Fig. 132. Start with the needle in the canvas just clear of the top of the rail and bring it out on the top side of the canvas about 1in short of the stuffing loops. Pull the needle through until its eye is only about 2in below the surface. Pivot the eye end of the needle round in an arc, at the same time pushing it back to come out approximately $\frac{1}{2}$in to the left of the first entry hole. This movement ensures that a fair amount of hair is caught up in the loop of the twine. Now draw the twine

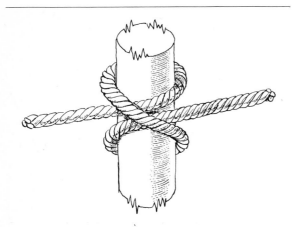

Fig. 133 The clove hitch.

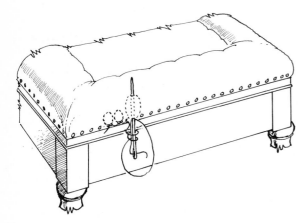

Fig. 134 Upholstery blind stitching.

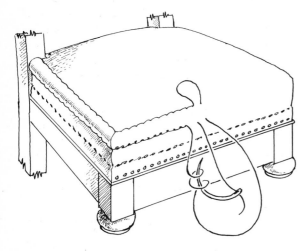

Fig. 135 Upholstery roll stitching.

through until only about 3in of its end protrudes from the first hole, tie this end with a clove hitch, Fig. 133, to the twine at the exit of the second hole and draw the twine tight thus bringing the hair within the twine loop firmly up to the side of the front canvas. Repeat this operation all the way round the seat, working from left to right, and looping the clove hitch over the end of the needle each time it exits at the seat rail. After the completion of the first loop, the needle is entered approximately 1in away from it and exits half an inch from it; that is ½in to the left of the entry hole. The next stitch starts 1in to the right of that entry hole and again exits ½in to the left of the entry hole. This is repeated round the complete frame, Fig. 134. After completing the row or rows of blind stitching, press with your hands on top of the canvas to check whether there is any unevenness in the stuffing. If there is it should be evened out with the regulator, Fig. 132.

The roll stitching can now be started. Using the curved needle, Fig. 132, enter it at the top front edge of the stuffing and, making sure that a fair amount of hair has been collected in the curve of the needle, bring it out at the top with approximately 2in of canvas between the entry and exit holes. Draw the twine through until about 3in remains at the entrance hole and then enter the needle in again ½in to the left of the exit hole and bring it out ½in to the left of the original entry hole. Draw the twine through and tie a clove hitch round it with the 3in piece left at the first entry hole. Now enter the needle ½in to the right of the original entry hole and bring it out ½in to the right of the original exit hole. Do not draw all the surplus twine through, only enough to work comfortably and re-enter the needle ½in to the left of the exit hole. That will be close to the original exit hole and bring it out close to the original entry hole. Loop a clove hitch over the needle with the surplus twine. The surplus twine can now be drawn through, tightening the stitching by nipping with the fingers above and below the roll as the twine is drawn tight. Enter the needle ½in to the right of the previous entry hole and repeat as before. This is continued round the complete frame, Fig. 135. A second row of stitching can be put through the centre of the roll if a very fine edge is required.

The top stuffing can now be applied on top of the canvas and inside the roll edge. It should be a fairly flat, firm layer of hair which is held in position by tucking it under the top loops. With the hair firm and even, a piece of calico is tacked over it temporarily. Make sure that it is pulled on evenly before fixing permanently. A double layer of upholstering wadding is then laid over the calico which has a skin on its face side which helps to stop the hair coming through. It is better if it is split and the two skin faces laid to the underside. The cover can now be fixed, and again it should be first temporarily tacked to make sure that it is even and, if it is a patterned material, to make sure that it is central. It is not necessary to tuck under the edges of the calico or those of the cover; they can be cut off with a sharp knife just short of the bottom of the rebate. The gimp or other trimming can now be glued on, and if there is a lot of shaping in the seat it may be necessary to tack it temporarily. When gluing trimming, tap with a hammer along its face to make sure the glue is holding it firmly. This should be done within a minute or so of gluing it down.

Spiral coil springing
The coil spring was used in England from about 1800 and about the same time deep-buttoning, which was later to be popular in the Victorian period, also came into use. Shallow-buttoning had been used in upholstery from about 1780.

Coil-sprung seat frames were made from timber approximately 2in × 2in in section instead of about 3in × 1¼in and the webbing was usually fixed on the underside instead of on top as for earlier upholstery. It is fairly obvious when an 18th century chair has been re-upholstered in the Victorian period using coil springs. The timber section is wrong and there will also be the old tack marks which fixed the webbing on the top of the rails. The piece should be converted back.

The early springs were thicker in gauge than those of the later periods, and instead of the ends of the springs being spiral-twisted round the

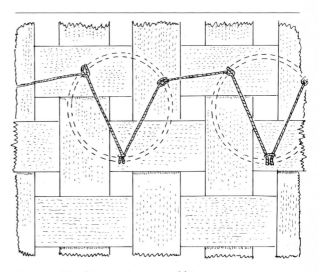

Fig. 136 Lashing springs to webbing.

spring wire itself, they were fixed in position by binding in very fine gauge wire. The webs for a sprung seat are spaced much closer than for a seat without springs. They should be not more than 1in apart and the springs should be fixed to the webbing with twine using three separate clove hitches looped round the lower ring of the springs, Fig. 136. With the lower end of the springs fixed in position the upper part of the springs should now be lashed with thick binder twine so that when they are compressed they keep true and do not buckle. Fix the end of the twine to a rail central to the first line of springs by entering a tack and looping the twine round the shank with a slip knot. Pull the knot tight and drive home the tack. Now fix the twine with a clove hitch to the near side of the top ring of the first spring, adjusting the length between the tack and the spring until, when the spring is compressed, the twine holds the top ring immediately over the bottom ring. When the spring is released it will be pulling over a little towards the rail. Take the twine across the centre of the top ring and tie a clove hitch on the opposite edge of the top ring. Take the twine to the next spring and tie with a clove hitch to the near and the far side of the top ring, making sure that the twine between the springs is just tight but not pulling the spring out of true. This is repeated over the row of springs treating the last spring in the same way as the first one. It is not necessary to tie off at the tack, the twine can

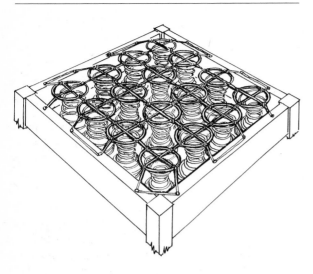

Fig. 137 Lashing tops of springs. The webbing is omitted to give the drawing clearer definition.

be looped round it and carried forward to be tacked down for the next row of springs. This lashing should be done, both from side to side and back to front, on all the lines of springs, Fig. 137. Canvas or hessian should now be laid over the springs and tacked to the rails. If a seat has springs fixed on top of the front rail these should be lashed to the rail independently and covered with a separate piece of canvas tacked to the back and top front edges of the rail. Sometimes a cane or thick wire is lashed to the top front edge of the rail springs and this should be retained. The hair should now be spread on the canvas to give a firm, flat and even surface and a second canvas fixed over it with a stitched top edge roll, the same as the springless seat. The hair ties are put in after this canvas is fixed. A layer of hair is then put on the top to slightly more than fill up to the level of the roll, and grey wadding laid over it before fixing the calico or cover.

Restoring metal fittings, reproductions and cleaning

When early iron fittings require restoration, or replacements are needed where parts are missing, it is advisable to get the local blacksmith to repair or make them. It is uneconomical for the restorer to do them himself, except for the very simple pieces such as a flat keyhole escutcheon. There are a number of suppliers who stock reproduction metal fittings, and it is advisable to have the catalogues of as many as possible to cover all the fittings available because they do not all carry the same period styles. It is also advisable to have the address of a small brass foundry for the replacement of cast fittings. Larger foundries are not usually prepared to produce one-off items.

If a fitting is missing and there is no matching reproduction, the restorer has no alternative than to make one. It is necessary, therefore, to have some sheet metal in stock, particularly 18 gauge brass for flat and fretted back plates and escutcheons, and 20 or 22 gauge for pressed or stamped metal plates. Making these specials is time-consuming work so it is essential that the value of the piece of furniture will justify it. It is usually possible to buy reproduction handle grips and bolts which will match or can be adjusted to do so, but if a handle grip is very ornate it can, of course, be ordered from the brass foundry by sending one of the originals as a pattern.

If the restorer intends to make the fret-edged or fretted and pierced flat back plates, he will need a jeweller's saw and piercing blades, or the blades alone fitted into a power jig-saw. If the plates are cut carefully and accurately they should not need any further fettling on the edges, but a set of needle files are useful if any adjustment is required. They should be used for bevelling or rounding the outside edges, although a certain amount of this can be done on a fine grinding wheel. When the shaping is finished the plate should be burnished to remove scratches, etc., using 0000 or 000 gauge wire wool, finishing with crocus or charcoal powder on an oily cloth. The bright surface of the plate will now need toning down and matching to the originals. If brass, this can be done by filling a flat tin box, big enough to allow the plate to lie flat, with American mahogany sawdust (Honduras or Brazilian). Pour a little full strength .880 ammonia between the side of the tin and the sawdust, just enough to cover the bottom of the tin. It must not wet the top layer of sawdust because if the ammonia touches the brass it will turn it black. The plate is then placed face down on the sawdust and left there long enough for it to be fumed to match the originals. It should then be polished with beeswax on a soft cloth.

If the plate is made from mild steel is should be dipped in a strong solution of caustic soda and left to dry naturally. It is then dipped in vinegar to neutralise the caustic and finally the surface should be polished with beeswax.

REPOUSSÉ WORK

A repoussé block is needed to reproduce stamped or pressed handle plates. This is made from 8 parts pitch, 8 parts plaster of Paris, 1 part tallow, $\frac{1}{2}$ part resin. Put the ingredients into a shallow roasting tin or similar, and melt and mix them

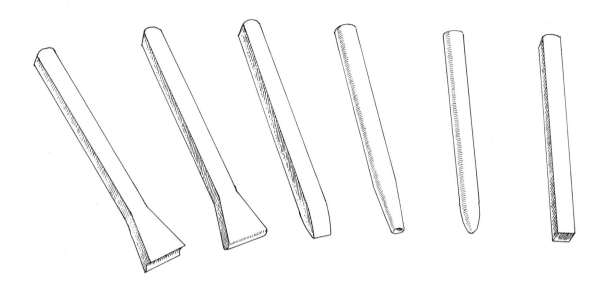

Fig 138 Punches for repoussé work.

over a flame until the liquid is smooth and even. Leave it to cool and set hard. From 20 or 22 gauge brass, cut a piece to the shape of one of the original handles, but a little larger to allow for the hollowing and shaping. Put the piece of brass over a flame to soften it, and while it is still hot lay it flat on the repoussé block, which will melt a little allowing the brass to sink level to its top surface. At the same time the repoussé will slightly overlap the metal edges so that it is held firmly when the repoussé sets. A variety of punches are required for working the brass to shape and these are usually made from brass or bronze by the craftsman himself. They can also be made from mild steel by the craftsman or by a blacksmith, Fig. 138. If the plate being copied is convex on its face, this is shaped with an engineer's dome-faced hammer; if it has reeding on it, the fluting punch is used; if a raised V-shape the V-punch is used and if it has beading on it, this should first be worked with the fluting punch. When the reverse side of the plate appears to be reasonably to shape it should be carefully eased off the repoussé block, reheated and put in a fresh place on the block, but this time with the face side up. Press down to make sure that the concave areas in the back are filled with the melting block. The reeding punch can now be used to correct any discrepancy in the

reed and if the plate has beading, the bead punch is used on the area already raised with the fluting punch. It is sometimes necessary to reverse the plate again and use the nosed punch to even up the bead. The grounding punch is used to true up any uneven surfaces, such as the one first worked with the dome-faced hammer. If the plate has raised floral or geometrical decoration on it, extra shaped punches may be required. When the shaping is completed the plate should be eased off the block and the surplus brass trimmed off the edges with a jeweller's piercing saw. The plate can now be cleaned and burnished with 0000 gauge wire wool, followed by crocus or charcoal powder and pressed level into the sawdust ammonia to colour. It should be finally polished with beeswax.

ENGRAVING

The engraving on a plate is, of course, best done with the correct tools for the job, but this is highly-skilled work and so for the inexperienced there are a number of small mechanical etchers on the market which work with a hammer action. These can be seen in use in department stores for engraving identity plates, etc. They are easy to use and turn out a reasonably satisfactory job if used slowly and with care. The engraving should be done before the plate is burnished and coloured. It is often possible to get a plain plate which matches the shape of the original from a reproduction suppliers. It is then only necessary for the restorer to do the engraving.

ORMOLU

Ormolu is gold on cast brass or bronze and was in use in France from the 16th century. English cast fittings, sometimes called ormolu, were not gilded until about the middle of the 18th century (the neo-classic period), but English furniture is occasionally seen with French mounts and fittings. The true ormolu was a process of mixing powdered gold with mercury (the two will amalgamate) and the mixture was then spread over the surface of the casting. When heated the mercury evaporated leaving the gold adhering to the casting. This process is now banned in England because it is poisonous and a danger to health.

Electro-plating is the process now used and although it is not so impervious to wear and tear as the original gilding, the general appearance is very good providing the casting has been cleanly fettled before plating. Old castings which have lost some of their gilt should not be electro-plated because this would destroy the finish of the original gilt, and it is most important that as much as possible of the original finish is retained. Patch restoration can be done by the restorer which, although not as permanent as the original ormolu, nevertheless will stand up to normal dusting and use and it is better than leaving it with the brass showing through.

With a beeswax block, rub over the area where the gold is missing. Burnish it with a soft brush until the wax appears to have disappeared completely and then immediately apply a layer of transfer-leaf gold to the surface, using a finger to press and rub it on. The gold will adhere to the thin layer of wax still left on the surface, and after leaving it for a period to allow the wax to really harden off, it can be polished with a soft cloth. A layer of beeswax and turpentine mixture

can be put over it and left to set before burnishing with a soft cotton cloth.

Repairs to brass fittings can usually be done by brazing but this should be put in the hands of a skilled craftsman who understands metals. Metal composition varies considerably and can have a very low melting point which, in unskilled hands, could mean that the fitting could be destroyed completely.

Old screws and pins should be retained wherever possible, and because they often vary in length and thickness, particularly when made by hand, it is necessary that they should be replaced in their original holes. A restorer known to the author, Charles K. Hole of Radnage Bucks., suggests keeping them in their correct order by threading them into a piece of cardboard as they are removed.

CONSERVING AND CLEANING METAL FITTINGS

The patina or surface finish on metal fittings is just as important as the finish on the timber surfaces and this should be retained whenever possible. Under no circumstances should wire wool be used to clean brass or copper fittings because it will scratch the surfaces and remove the natural colour layer which it is important to retain. There are a number of different techniques which may be used for cleaning brass and copper without destroying their surface finish.

Lemon juice will remove superficial dirt, cut the lemon in half and rub it over the dirty surface, leave the juice on for a short period and then remove it with a cotton cloth.

Washing soda in hot water will remove dirt from badly discoloured fittings but the surfaces should then be washed over with vinegar to neutralise the soda. The fittings must be removed from the furniture when using soda or it will damage the wood surface finish.

Very dirty fittings may be cleaned by soaking them in a solution of hot water and household washing powder. When they are removed they should be washed with clean water and waxed.

If the fittings are very dirty and covered with verdigris, they should be immersed completely in full-strength liquid ammonia and soaked for about half an hour. When they are removed they must immediately be immersed in clean hot water. If they are not immersed completely in both the ammonia and also the water, they will turn black. Holding them below the water they can now be scrubbed with a soft brush until they are clean. Finally immerse them in vinegar to make sure that any ammonia which may be left is neutralised. Any ammonia left on will turn the brass black.

All fittings that have been treated should be polished with beeswax to prevent them discolouring again.

A guide to estimating

The restorer should carefully check each piece of furniture before starting on any restoration, and carefully list all repairs which are required. A list of these repairs should be passed to the customer, together, if required, with an approximate estimate of the cost. It is almost impossible for the inexperienced eye to realise the extent of the work required, and when the restoration has been completed no sign of the repairs should be noticeable.

The following is a guide for examination of the furniture and the approximate time required for doing the repairs, these times are average and do not take into consideration the difference in speed of individual craftsmen and their experience.

The times include selection and preparation of materials although they do not appear to be shown in the guide, for example, the time shown for making joints on the carcases also includes preparing and selecting the timber, see page 111.

The times shown are for one off work. Time is deducted for more than one as shown on page 111.

Carcases
Every joint in a carcase should be estimated at 2 hours per joint, this includes mortice and tenon, dovetails, dowels, mitres, housings, etc. It also includes edge to edge joints whether they be tongued and grooved, dowelled or rubbed joints.

Dovetailed carcase joints which are over a foot wide should be estimated at 2 hours per foot, and any part of a foot to count as a foot, for

example, 6in wide = 2 hours and 1ft 6in = 4 hours.

Mitre or double-lap dovetailing (secret dovetails) should be increased by a $\frac{1}{2}$ hour per foot, or part of a foot.

Mouldings
Estimate plain moulding at $\frac{1}{2}$ hour per foot up to 2in wide, and carved moulding at 2 hours per foot up to 2in wide and add 1 hour for every extra 2in or part of 2in of width. These times are for moulding on table tops, carcases, legs, rails, doors, drawer fronts, cornices, plinths, etc. Add $\frac{1}{2}$ hour per foot for curved or serpentine moulded shapes.

Veneering
Estimate at 1 hour per square foot for laying by hand or press, cross-banding will take $\frac{1}{2}$ hour per foot, and inlay lines up to $\frac{1}{2}$in wide at $\frac{1}{2}$ hour per foot, or over $\frac{1}{2}$in wide to 1 hour per foot.

Turning
Estimate at 1 hour per foot up to 2in thick, any part of a foot to count as a foot, minimum charge one hour. Add 1 hour per foot per 2in of diameter. For reeds, flutes or other moulding on turnings, estimate as for mouldings taking the circumference as the width of the mould.

Drawers
Estimate 8 hours per drawer, this includes making the drawer complete, fitting runners, kickers and running in (fitting) the drawer.

Fitting handles would be extra. Cockbeads should be estimated at $\frac{1}{2}$ hour per foot plus $\frac{1}{2}$ hour per joint. Moulding planted on drawers should be estimated as moulding plus $\frac{1}{2}$ hour for each joint.

Doors
Estimate 4 hours per door for fitting, hanging and fixing hinges and locks. Making a door should be estimated as for carcase work, for example, 2 hours per joint; 1 hour per foot, for plain moulding, or 2 hours for carved; jointing in panel at 1 hour per foot and veneering at 1 hour per square foot. Tracery work should be estimated at 2 hours per glass panel in addition to moulding and framework.

Laminates
For shaped doors, drawers, and carcase ends, etc., the construction should be estimated at 8 hours per square foot, making a 5% reduction per door, drawer, or carcase for two or more of matching shape up to a maximum of 30%.

Backs
Framed backs should be estimated as for doors, plus 2 hours for fitting and fixing.

Shelves
Estimate at 1 hour per shelf for fitting and fixing.

Tops
Estimate the fixing of tops to carcases at 1 hour per top. Leather or baize on tops would be 1 hour per square foot for preparation and laying.

Legs
Estimate pad foot cabriole legs at 2 hours per leg, and claw and ball, lion paw, or scroll at 5 hours per leg (complete with wings). Estimate moulded legs as for moulding multiplied by number of moulded sides to the leg. For turned legs see turning, which also includes fluted or reeded legs. Estimate knee carvings (acanthus leaf, shell, etc.) at maximum of 4 hours each.

Carving
This can be estimated on the same basis as carving on knees, 4 hours maximum for each leaf or rosette, etc.

Rule joints
Estimate as for two mouldings (1 hour per foot) plus fitting and hinging at 1 hour per foot, making a total of 2 hours per foot.

Knuckle joints
Estimate at 2 hours per joint to 1 foot in length, and 2 hours for any foot or part of a foot in excess of this (a joint 2ft 6in = 6 hours).

Polishing
Times include glass papering, staining, filling the grain and other colourings, etc.

Full gloss finish should be estimated at 2 hours per foot and full matt finish at 1 hour per square foot. Coating and wax finishing at $\frac{1}{2}$ hour per square foot.

Plain moulding up to 2in wide, full polished $\frac{1}{4}$ hour per foot, plus $\frac{1}{8}$ hour for every 2in or part of 2in over.

Carved moulding up to 2in wide, fully polished $\frac{3}{4}$ hour per foot, plus $\frac{3}{4}$ hour for every 2in or part of 2in over in width.

Carving on panels, pilasters, frames and other reasonably flat surfaces should be calculated at $2\frac{1}{4}$ hours per square foot of full polished surface.

Carving in the round, fully polished, should be estimated at 2 hours per square foot of surface area.

Turnings up to 2in in diameter should take 1 hour per foot of length for full polishing, plus $\frac{1}{2}$ hour for every additional inch or part of 1in in the size of the diameter, for example a leg 30in × 3in diameter = $3\frac{3}{4}$ hours.

The notes below refer to estimating for renewal of missing constructional parts only, and not to the general repairs which follow.

The time rate for all items is for one-off only and includes making patterns, selecting timber, cutting, shaping and finishing. If more than one is made, 5% per item (to the nearest half hour) is deductable, up to a maximum of $33\frac{1}{3}$%.

Examples

4 legs @ 2 hours = 8 hours less $4 \times 5\% = 20\%$ (say $1\frac{1}{2}$ hours) = $6\frac{1}{2}$ hours

5 drawers @ 8 hours = 40 hours, less $5 \times 5\%$ = 25% (10 hours) = 30 hours

2 bottom carcase dovetail joints 18ins wide @ 4 hours per joint = 8 hours, $2 \times 5\%$ = 10% (say 1 hour) = 7 hours

8 drawer rail and muntin joints = 16 hours less $33\frac{1}{3}\% = 5\frac{1}{2}$ hours = $10\frac{1}{2}$ hours

4 top rail joints = 8 hours less $4 \times 5\% = 20\%$ ($1\frac{1}{2}$ hours) = $6\frac{1}{2}$ hours

Moulding top $5\frac{1}{2}$ feet (say 6 feet) = 3 hours less $6 \times 5\% = 30\%$ (1 hour) = 2 hours

8 base frame joints = 16 hours less $33\frac{1}{3}\%$ (say $5\frac{1}{2}$ hours) = $10\frac{1}{2}$ hours

Moulding base mould and jointing (say 6ft) = 3 hours less 30% (1 hour) = 2 hours and 4 joints = 8 hours, less 20% ($1\frac{1}{2}$ hours) = $6\frac{1}{2}$ hours

Fixing top and back @ 2 hours each = 4 hours

ESTIMATING REPAIRS ONLY, INCLUDING EXAMINATION PROCEDURE

It is possible to standardise this only to a certain extent, sometimes special allowances have to be made, so this is a guide only.

Repairs not classed as construction or veneering

Deep bruising requiring damp and heat treatment, $\frac{1}{2}$ hour per bruise per square inch.

Fitting, fixing and colouring small pieces missing out of solid surfaces, 1 hour per piece.

Restoring missing pieces of carving, 1 hour per square inch plus $\frac{1}{2}$ hour for every additional square inch or part.

Small pieces of gesso and gilt, $\frac{3}{4}$ hour per 2 square inches or part.

Missing gilt only, $\frac{1}{4}$ hour per 2 square inches or part, for example 3 square inches of gesso and gilt = $1\frac{1}{2}$ hours, or 5 square inches of missing gilt only = $\frac{3}{4}$ hour.

Veneered and marquetry furniture

Laying blisters, up to 9 square inches $\frac{1}{2}$ hour, over 9 square inches = $\frac{1}{2}$ hour for first 9 square inches plus $\frac{1}{4}$ hour for every additional 9 square inches or part. For example, 5 square inches = $\frac{1}{2}$ hour; 16 square inches = $\frac{3}{4}$ hour; two blisters at 7 square inches each = 1 hour.

Restoring missing veneer. Each piece up to one foot square = 1 hour or pieces with area of more than one square foot = 1 hour per foot or part therefore. For example, $2\frac{3}{8}$ square feet = 3 hours.

Restoring marquetry. Relaying blisters in marquetry, time as for veneer. Restoring missing marquetry with area of less than 9 square inches $\frac{1}{2}$ hour per piece of design plus 1 hour for area. If over 9 square inches, add 1 hour for each additional 9 square inches or part plus $\frac{1}{2}$ hour for each piece of design. For example, 17 square inches, which includes five pieces of veneer in the design = $4\frac{1}{2}$ hours.

Restoring buhl, etc. Relaying brass, tortoiseshell, mother of pearl, pewter, marble, etc. Area of 9 square inches or less = 1 hour per section plus $\frac{1}{2}$ hour per piece.

Area over 9 square inches = 1 hour per 9 square inches plus 1 hour for each 9 inches or part thereof, plus $\frac{1}{2}$ hour for each separate piece in the area. For example, 24 square inches with 16 pieces in the design would be 3 hours for the area plus 8 hours for the pieces = 11 hours total.

Restoring missing buhl. Area of 9 square inches or less = $1\frac{1}{2}$ hours per section plus $1\frac{1}{2}$ hours for each new piece fitted. Area over 9 square inches = $1\frac{1}{2}$ hours per 9 square inches, plus $1\frac{1}{2}$ hours for each 9 inches or part thereof plus $1\frac{1}{2}$ hours for each new piece fitted. For example, 33 square inches with 11 pieces in the design would be 6 hours for the area plus $16\frac{1}{2}$ hours for the pieces = $22\frac{1}{2}$ hours total.

Repairs to chairs and stools

Examination should always be in the same rotation to avoid missing anything (back, sides, front, underside).

Check head rail for loose or broken joints. Check arms and wings for loose or broken joints. Check back seat rail joints, first with your knee on seat and hand on top of back, lever lightly to check whether any joints are loose.

Check other seat frame joints by taking hold of two legs at a time and levering lightly for loose joints. With one hand at seat rail joint and other hand holding a corresponding leg, lever up and down for breakages of joints under the upholstery. Check stretchers for loose or broken joints.

Estimate as follows.
Refixing joints which are loose only $\frac{1}{2}$ hour per joint.
If joints which are firm need to be disjointed for convenience of repairing other joints, time them as for loose joints $\frac{1}{2}$ hour per joint.
Rejointing cracks (in top of legs, or in rails, splat, etc.) $\frac{1}{2}$ hour per crack.
Repairing broken joints, 2 hours per joint.
New seat frame blocks, on shaped seat frame, 1 hour per block; on square seat frame, $\frac{1}{2}$ hour per block.

For restoring missing pieces see page 111.

Removing and refixing upholstery as required for repairs
Remove and re-seat complete with stitched border, 7 hours plus 1 hour for trimmings.
Remove and re-seat complete without border, 5 hours plus trimmings.
Top stuffing only with border, 3 hours plus trimmings.
Top stuffing only without border, 2 hours plus trimmings.
Half length stuffover back complete, 3 hours plus trimmings.
Half length pin cushion back complete, 3 hours plus trimmings.
Full length pin cushion back complete, 5 hours plus trimmings.
Full length stuffover back complete, 5 hours plus trimmings.
Close brass nailing using old nails, 1 hour per foot.
Close brass nailing using new nails, $\frac{1}{2}$ hour per foot.

Remake arm pads complete, 5 hours per chair.
Remake stuffover arms complete, 8 hours per chair.
Stuffover arms cover only, 4 hours per chair.
Wings stuff and cover completely, 5 hours per chair.
Wings top cover only, 3 hours per chair.

Repairs to cabinets, tables and stands
Examination rotation should be top, back, sides, base, interiors, front. Tables and stands can be checked for loose joints in the same way as chairs, by light leverage of the legs. Cabinets may be checked for loose joints by pressure across the front diagonal of the carcase at the same time holding a finger across each joint to detect any movement; framed doors may be checked in the same way. Bases, boxes and drawers may be checked by pressure across the top diagonal.

Constructional breakages such as a broken leg should be estimated as for making a joint (2 hours) unless the damage requires a new piece splicing into it, then it should be calculated as two joints (4 hours).

If a cabriole leg is broken and part missing it should be calculated as for making a complete leg, but no extra allowance should be made for jointing (for example, a pad foot = 2 hours; a ball and claw foot = 5 hours).

Plinth feet should be estimated as two joints which includes jointing, shaping, and fixing (4 hours), if only one half of the foot is missing allow 2 hours. If the plinth foot has a toe on it 2 hours extra should be allowed which will include veneering the complete foot.

Rejointing carcase, backs, sides and tops, drawer bottoms, etc. All loose joints up to one foot in length = 1 hour per joint and $\frac{1}{2}$ hour for each extra foot of jointing or part over 12 inches.

If joints which are firm need to be disjointed, for convenience of repairing other joints, they should be timed as for loose joints.

Cracks which require filling, up to one foot in length = 1 hour plus 1 hour for each extra foot or part of a foot. Cracks which can be closed up should be estimated at $\frac{1}{2}$ hour per foot plus $\frac{1}{2}$ hour for extra foot or part.

When calculating all repairs allowance has been made for colouring and polishing them, but if a complete area requires repolishing, it should be estimated separately (see polishing).

These times should be used as a guide only, and are based on the average speed of work. Accurate time records should be kept when doing the work so that adjustments can be made to suit individual speeds and requirements. Allowance has been made in these times for sorting out and selecting materials and this should be included in the time-recording.

Opposite and near right:
This Thomas Tompion walnut long-case clock had
had its lower, worm-eaten section supported by fixing
on it a wide oak plinth. To repair it, this was
removed and the background restored by filling the
worm-eaten timber with plaster of Paris and glue
size. The panels were then made up again with
matching veneer and a new plinth of the correct size
was made and fixed.

Far right and below:
Most of the marquetry and the plinth was missing
from this clock base and had to be replaced. The
damage was probably the result of standing on a damp
stone floor.

This walnut drop-front secretaire had obviously been affected by damp or worm and the base section had been replaced with oak plinth feet. The dividing mould had also been replaced in oak. These were restored back to the original with ball feet and walnut crossband moulds.

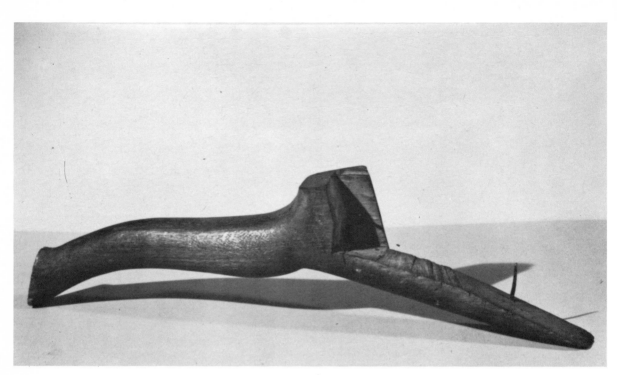

Opposite:
The left back leg on this settee was renewed,
replacing a very crude earlier repair.

Below:
As a result of being stored in a damp place sections
of the cross-band cornice mould and the front veneers
were missing. The base mould and the ball feet were
also missing. The restored cabinet is shown with the
metal fittings cleaned or replaced.

The veneers on this card or gaming table were loose as a result of the background shrinking. The blocks at the top of the legs also had to be refitted and fixed for the same reason.

Opposite:
This mahogany and parcel gilt 18th century chair had been over-painted green with the carving painted in bronze-powder paint. When these were removed, a large percentage of the original gold leaf and polish was revealed.

As a result of incorrect re-upholstery the swan-neck friezes had been broken. Some had been forced off by the upholstery when the stool was in use, and were missing completely. The renewals show white in the illustration. The friezes were removed, the stool correctly upholstered and the friezes replaced.

This James II stool is part of a suite comprising two chairs and six stools. They had been over-painted with black lacquer and when the lacquer was removed the original parcel silver and gilt was revealed. Parts of the carving such as birds, cherub's arms and sheaths of arrows were also missing which may have been the reason for the piece being lacquered over.

This chair was so damaged and had been so badly repaired in the past that it would have been uneconomic to restore it, except for the fact that it was one of a set of eight and all the others were in reasonable condition.

The rosettes were carved on a paper-board from which they can easily be removed.

This painted and parcel gilt suite was designed by Adam for the house in which it stands, unfortunately a number of the carved rosettes were missing and had to be replaced. The covers of cherry red and green silk brocade were so dilapidated that they also had to be replaced, but there was enough of the original for them to be accurately copied.

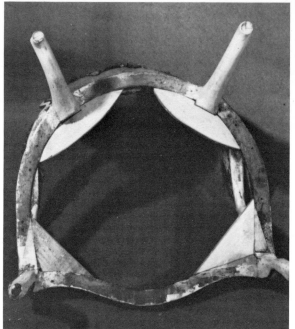

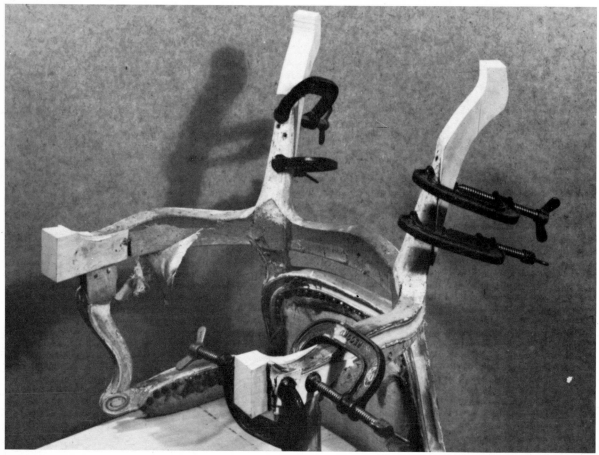

This chair, one of a set, had been weakened by worm and the side rail joints had broken away from the front legs. The back legs had parts spliced on to them, but had been further weakened by screwing the glued joints. The timbers were strengthened with glue size before splicing out the rails for new tenons, and splicing out the legs.

This chair, which was one of a set, had been badly weakened by worm and was injected with glue size and strengthened so that all the original could be retained. The wood had also been overpainted and grained to resemble dark walnut. This was removed to display the original colour and decoration underneath it.

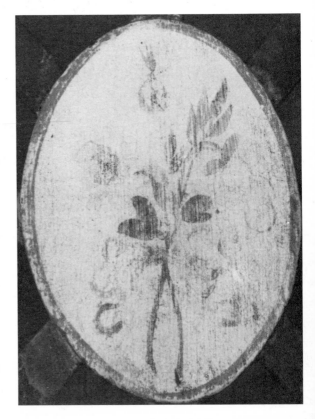

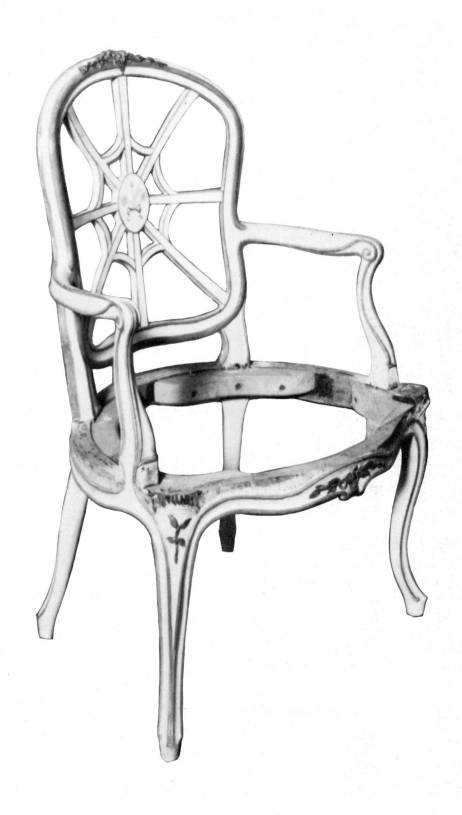

This suite of Adam period chairs had been altered in the Victorian period by painting over the picture panels on the headrails and applying a gilded carving over them. The borders had been covered with gold leaf. When the false finishes were removed, the pictures showed cream coloured figures on a pale blue background depicting various activities such as fishing, navigation, dancing, play, etc. The borders were cherry-red with a pearl polka dot enclosed by gilded beads.

The single chair which made the suite complete was found in an attic with the front legs broken off at the rails and missing. Also the picture on the headrail through still discernible had to be repainted in tempera.

This chair, one of a set, was weakened by worm and damaged. It was restored using the same method as that used for the chair on page 128.

Index